P9-DXZ-189

Dynamics of Counterrevolution in Europe,
1870–1956

Dynamics of Counterrevolution in Europe, 1870-1956:

An Analytic Framework

ARNO J. MAYER

HARPER TORCHBOOKS
Harper & Row, Publishers
New York, Evanston, San Francisco, London

DYNAMICS OF COUNTERREVOLUTION IN EUROPE, 1870–1956

Copyright © 1971 by Arno J. Mayer. All rights reserved. Printed in the United States of America. No part of this book may be used or reproduced without written permission except in the case of brief quotations embodied in critical articles and reviews. For information address Harper & Row, Publishers, Inc., 49 East 33rd Street, New York, New York 10016. Published simultaneously in Canada by Fitzhenry and Whiteside Limited, Toronto.

First TORCHBOOK edition published 1971.

LIBRARY OF CONGRESS CATALOG CARD NUMBER: 77–145684

STANDARD BOOK NUMBER: 06–131579–6

for Aline

Contents

Part One: Setting

Part Two: Framework

Part Three: Questions

Contents

Part One: Setting

Preface
1. Ideological and Cultural Context
2. Some Preliminary Distinctions

Part Two: Framework

3. Counterrevolution: A Heuristic Concept
4. Varieties of Counterrevolution

Part Three: Questions

5. Reflections on Counterrevolution
6. Internal Causes and Purposes of War
Selected Bibliography

part one

Setting

Preface

To probe into counterrevolution is to venture onto treacherous ground. The word-concept "counterrevolution" carries a considerable political and emotional load. The establishment dislikes it because of its censorious connotations, and left-wing dissenters embrace it for its critical thrust. Because it is so politically charged, historians and social scientists tend to shy away from it, insisting on its incompatibility with their value-free labors.

But to proscribe the word-concept "counterrevolution" and to evade its clarification is not to eschew but to take a political position. Advocates of terminological and conceptual neutrality unwittingly perpetuate scholarly as well as political ignorance about vital aspects of contemporary history. Not altogether fortuitously, this ignorance surrounds historical developments to which their own government and society contribute but about which they prefer to avoid or to mute critical debate.

The writer of this essay is a confirmed leftist critic of those Allied and American policies, both foreign and domestic, that condoned or advanced, intentionally or unintentionally, the counterrevolutionary side in the era of the communist revolution. As such, he believes that the harm of continuing ignorance, contrived silence, or specious neutrality about counterrevolution by far exceeds the danger of squarely facing up to its *problématique*.

Accordingly, the purpose behind this heuristic concept of counterrevolution is to advance the critical examination, understanding, and debate of contemporary history. There is no hidden or subordinate desire to contribute to purely deductive social theory or to practical policy prescription, which are both the business and the bane of the social and behavioral sciences.

The research design for any such sensitive undertaking is bound to be biased. Valuational presuppositions inevitably inform not only one's definition of purpose but also one's principles

1

of inclusion and exclusion. Whereas some scholars consider these normative or teleological imperatives undesirable obstacles to their work, others hail them as welcome though beguiling lodestars for research. But whatever view one takes of this eternal issue, it may be wisest to proceed by explicitly confessing one's most relevant biases.

Among the valuations underlying this heuristic concept of counterrevolution perhaps the following should be mentioned: that the two extremes of the political spectrum are not identical; that revolution is more productive of human growth, betterment, and dignity than counterrevolution; that political, economic, and social structures and conjunctures rather than innate psychological drives determine political behavior in crisis situations; that in such crises counterrevolutionary ideas are weapons of infinite malleability; and that counterrevolution is the product of a constellation of world history and not of localized national aberrations.

In elaborating this construct I have made every effort to check the distorting influences of these subjective valuations. Throughout, loaded language has been avoided by recourse to the "neutral" vocabulary of the social sciences. Also, in order to allow for wide ranges of significant variations, most hypothesized uniformities have been heavily qualified.

Still, no matter how deliberate and painstaking, this effort at value neutralization remains circumscribed by the politically charged subject to which it is directed. Specifically, there is no corrective for the value-laden decisions as to which aspects of counterrevolution to explore, emphasize, or ignore.

Such preliminary questions are formulated during an initial conceptual stocktaking: to see the counterrevolutionary phenomenon as one whole while at the same time seeing the interrelations and linkages among its multiple components. In other words, the facts and ideas of the counterrevolutionary phenomenon do not organize themselves. A systematic framework rather than unstructured observation imparts meaning and coherence to the welter of raw data.

Any framework, in addition to being valuationally conditioned, is bound and intended to be tentative. It is formulated in the midst of reading and research and is premised on further empirical verification and correction. In the meantime, however, it serves its purpose: through questions and hypotheses it provides criteria of relevance and significance with which to dissect the counterrevolutionary phenomenon into its component parts, which, in turn, are laid out for historical analysis.

A construct is not to be mistaken for an explication of concrete reality. Rather, it is designed to be a guide in the quest for historical explanation. The greatest merit (or drawback?) of this particular construct is that it systematically stresses certain characteristics and tendencies of the counterrevolutionary phenomenon—e.g., its reactionary and conservative coordinates and its pre-emptive bent—that strike me, but not necessarily others, as central. But there is, of course, the hazard, which is notorious in the writing of conceptual history, of forcing the data to fit the construct.

There is no way of avoiding this pitfall altogether. Even historians who defiantly reject any conceptual approach in favor of indeterminate multi-factor analysis tend to force their explanations. Usually their brash refusal to rank different factors in some meaningful order of importance is in the nature of an implicit, if not explicit, contra-position to the single-factor economic interpretation of history. Today's historians still like to begin their studies with simplistic versions or, more commonly, outright caricatures of the economic interpretations they mean to destroy. They also would have their readers believe that concepts and methods of analysis remain constant, or that to the extent that they develop, they become not only more accurate but also value-free.

Obviously, today's historians do, indeed, have the use of new and sharper concepts and methods; and these enable them to explore questions that were beyond the reach of their predecessors, whatever their biases. But, in turn, these new approaches are conditioned and limited by the valuations underlying the scholarship and intellection of later days.

For example, current concentration on social history is the outgrowth of an ideologically conditioned retreat from preoccupation with the critical nexus of economics and politics. At the same time, it is fostered and legitimized by developments in

quantitative methods of analysis. One need not question or
distrust the impressive contributions of quantification to historical studies in order to stress its paradigmatic limitations: it
fixes attention on problems of socioeconomic history that lend
themselves to statistical measurement. Along the way this focus
excludes attention to political questions, as well as to the critical
interplay between socioeconomic and political structures and
developments. Of course, it also so happens that political events
that are inseparable from economic, social, and ideational developments yield much less readily to serial and correlational
numerical statements. They require attention to discrete and
short-term conjunctures as well as to the qualitative dimensions
of motive, purpose, and feeling.

In any case, the study of counterrevolution calls for an advance
to concern with <u>causal interconnections</u> between aggregate socioeconomic and ideational developments on the one hand and,
on the other, distinct political actions and events. Wherever
meaningful and possible, quantification must be pressed into
service. But important issues and linkages cannot be ignored
or dismissed simply because they resist explanation by numerical
referents.

Counterrevolution is not a phenomenon of political, economic,
or social equilibrium. It does not surface in stationary and stable
societies. In fact, <u>counterrevolution is a product and stimulant of
instability, cleavages, and disorders.</u> It thrives when normally
conflictual but accommodating forces begin to abandon the
politics of compromise.

A <u>structural-functional approach is too confining and static</u> for
the study of this crisis politics, which is at the core of the counterrevolutionary phenomenon. Structural-functionalists conceive
of economy, society, and polity as an integrated system whose
component parts are designed to secure its orderly survival. To
the extent that they allow for change, they consider it to be not
only gradual but also susceptible to assimilation <u>into a moving</u>
equilibrium.

<u>Crisis politics</u> simply will not fit into such a constricting analytic
frame. It will only yield to a framework that can handle conditions
of consequential instability. These conditions stem from conflicts

between individuals, strata, and organizations that refuse to be or remain integrated into an equilibrated system of functionally related and serviceable interdependent parts. Students of crisis politics need multi-angled and adjustable lenses with which to examine such unsettled situations. These lenses must be able to focus on the narrow synchronic and the broad diachronic aspects of explosive conjunctures as well as on the intersections between them.

The conflict or violence that accompanies this disaggregation is intrinsic rather than extrinsic to any national situation and system, including the interactions of this situation and system with the international environment. To grapple with this amalgam of simultaneous change, conflict, and violence it is necessary to combine temporal and homeostatic analysis. Both structural-functionalists and behavioralists will have to yield to social scientists who consider history as past politics and politics as current history and who have a dynamic, analytic, and comparative rather than a static, descriptive, and national conception of the links between history and politics.

My close friend Felix Gilbert prompted me to make this foray into conceptualization. It was he who asked me to clarify, for him, the sense in which I used the word counterrevolution in the subtitle and text of my last book.[1] I gave a preliminary answer in a paper discussed at a colloquium of the history faculties of Princeton University and the neighboring Institute for Advanced Study. In the course of an unforgettable and crushing evening, my colleagues took turns telling me that I had no subject, that I was merely giving another label to German nazism, that there were no essential differences between sovietism and nazism, that counterrevolution was simply opposition to revolution, and that in any case historians had no business conceptualizing.

I nearly gave up on the problem, except that my current research and teaching would not let me. In both I am concerned with an analytically and topically structured study of the political and diplomatic history of Europe in the era 1870 to 1956. Where-

DYNAMIC — ANALYTIC — COMPARATIVE

[1] *Politics and Diplomacy of Peacemaking: Containment and Counterrevolution at Versailles, 1918–1919* (New York: Knopf, 1967).

as the revolutionary developments of those years have been thoroughly examined, the same cannot be said about the "antirevolutionary" side. There are few solid secondary sources on such major topics as the repression of the Paris Commune in 1871; the nascent mass movements from the right of the last quarter of the nineteenth century; the political mainsprings of the new imperialism, the internal security systems and operations of the major European countries after 1890; the social carriers, politics, and mechanics of the antirevolution, including the pogroms in Russia, 1905–1917; the profile and actions of the Ulster movement, the growth, configuration, and interplay of far-rightist ideas and political carriers before and during the First World War; the "liberation" of Munich and Hungary in 1919, including the white terror; the project and terror of the Whites in the Russian civil war, 1917 to 1920; the strategies of bourgeois defense against mounting revolutionary and advanced reformist pressures between the wars; the attitudes and policies of reactionaries and conservatives toward the rise of fascism; the domestic taproots of the diplomacy of appeasement; collaborationism in wartime Europe; and the political dynamics of the containment of communism and advanced reformism this side of the Oder-Neisse line after the Second World War.

The cumulative effect of encountering so many unexamined developments and events of striking family resemblances was to spur me on to revise and expand my original essay. I needed and still need a preliminary road map to guide the exploration of this neglected "other" side of the history of our times, a map that many of my students at Princeton and Columbia have urged me to make available to others.

Chapter 6 of this book is a reprint of a previously published conceptual scheme for the study of the domestic causes and purposes of war in the same historical era. In addition to raising some general issues about the phenomenon of war, it points to the links between counterrevolution and external belligerency that are touched on in the preceding chapters and that call for closer scrutiny.

Finally, I have resisted two temptations. The first was to so shape the construct as to also take account of the counterrevolu-

- he does not mean it to apply to 3rd World

tionary aspects of the containment and repression of independence and national liberation movements in the Third World. Others will have to wrestle with these facets of decolonization. To do so here would involve diluting the heuristic construct, leaving it with a blunted cutting edge for the study of developments both in the Third World and in Europe.

The second temptation was to comment on the current American scene. Any student of counterrevolution must halt before the upsurge of the far right in a callous imperial polity and society whose disaggregation is simultaneously being stayed and quickened by a formidable military-industrial complex and its concomitant international truculence. But the words and deeds of Agnew, Reagan, and Wallace, as well as of their associates, patrons, and supporters, are so unambiguous that they explain themselves. Besides, this conceptual construct is designed as an aid to the study of an era that closed in 1956; and it was formulated before the "other" side of recent developments in the United States became so stridently visible. Should this construct nevertheless contribute to a critical understanding and discussion of the unfolding situation in America, I hope that the fit of the shoe will never become too perfect.

A. J. M.

Summer, 1970

1. Ideological and Political Context

Counterrevolution is closely interlocked with revolution. In fact, the two are symbiotically related. To concede the historical reality of the one is to concede the historical reality of the other. In the context of contemporary world history any such concession calls for the acknowledgment that the communist revolution —first in its Russian and then in its Chinese phase—is the central event of this era. Accordingly, the outside—not to say the surrounding—world measured and continues to measure itself against this revolutionary model; it also reacted and continues to react with policies of containment, both domestic and foreign.

Needless to say, containment is not equivalent to counterrevolution, as Moscow and Peking intermittently charge for their own political and diplomatic purposes. At the international level there are important differences between defensive, pre-emptive, and offensive containment, just as on the domestic level there are important differences between reaction,[1] conservatism,[2] and counterrevolution.[3] But the point to note is that at critical moments these varieties of countermovement interpenetrate each other both internationally and domestically, with the result that counterrevolutionary ingredients enter into even the mildest amalgam of international and domestic containment.

And yet these counterrevolutionary determinants, objectives, and consequences of the confrontation with the communist revolution have tended to be ignored, minimized, or concealed. Certainly, they have not been closely scrutinized. From a world perspective America emerged first, between 1917–1920, as the linchpin and then, as of 1944, as the mainstay of containment in the international civil war of the twentieth century. Even so, her leaders and action intellectuals never avowed, let alone

[1] See pp. 48–49.
[2] See pp. 49–55.
[3] See Chapter 3.

9

advertised, any of the reactionary, restorative, or counterrevolutionary impulses and implications of America's domestic and foreign policies.

The degree to which this evasion or dissimulation was intended and conscious remains uncertain. But whatever the degree of deliberate intent this much seems clear: in an age of mass and ideological politics even reactionary, conservative, and counterrevolutionary governments project a populist, reformist, and emancipatory image of their purposes. That successive American administrations should have done so is only natural. The ideology of the liberating world crusade against totalitarian bolshevism drew sustenance from America's carefully nurtured and blazoned self-image of a nation endowed with a congenital yet benign revolutionary heritage, and mission. Admittedly, this crusade produced reactionary, restorative, and counterrevolutionary effects in third countries. But whenever these became too blatant to be disputed or glossed over, they were rationalized away as a small price to pay for keeping communism in check.

As for the conservative domestic taproots, purposes, and consequences of overseas containment, these were mitigated by the general economic prosperity of the postwar decades. In addition, almost as if to deflect attention from these conservative coordinates, America's mythmakers proclaimed the breakthrough into mass consumption to be part of a broad-gauged permanent revolution of primary benefit to the common man. Without major changes in political, economic, and class structures, the establishment was said to be presiding over a liberating and elevating kitchen revolution, corporate revolution, computer revolution, transportation revolution, paperback revolution, and sex revolution. It was only a short step from strident self-congratulation for this politically innocuous "revolution" at home to eager encouragement of "the revolution of rising expectations" abroad. Naturally, to be sanctified by Washington, this "revolutionary" process abroad would have to proceed by compromise and consensus, without perilous political and social disruptions.

With pluralistic and consensual politics as the new norm and paradigm, revolution and counterrevolution were factored out for being two essentially identical sides of monolithic totalitarianism. Not only ideologists but also scholars proclaimed that the two extremes of the political spectrum touch each other in all essential aspects. Revolution and counterrevolution were said to be similar not only in consequences but also in political origins, in social carriers, in the personality of actors, in methods, in organization, in style, and in objectives. Presently, with the help of the concept of totalitarianism, surface similarities between Soviet Communism and German National Socialism were transmuted into basic identities, with the result that communism and fascism became virtually undistinguishable.

In retrospect, and in the overheated ideological climate of the Cold War, this hypostatized identity of communism and fascism achieved high scholarly as well as political credibility and usefulness. But while fascism progressed and triumphed in Italy and Germany, and while fascist or fascoid forces and influences pervaded other European countries and Japan, contemporaries saw these developments from an altogether different perspective. In the twenties and thirties, not to mention the years of the Grand Alliance, communism and fascism stood out as polar opposites calling for a clear if painful choice. In some instances the mere refusal, reluctance, or inability to make that choice had momentous historical consequences. On the international level the costs of indetermination became particularly dramatic and were driven home by the diplomacy of appeasement, beginning with the Spanish Civil War and culminating in the Munich agreement and the Nazi-Soviet pact.

In addition to countless waverers and fence sitters, there were legions of reactionary and conservative political actors who, without too much hesitation, proceeded to collaborate with the fascists. Admittedly, at first most of them did so in a spirit of calculated expediency. Confident of their ability to control fascist energies, they meant to harness these to a countermovement that was directed as much against the general modernizing thrusts of history that began with the French Revolution as against either Soviet Russia or the communist parties of their respective countries. Before long, however, these opportunistic collaborators discovered that fascism was not a surgical instrument, to be discarded with impunity following their own preservative and restorative operations. By the late thirties Hermann Rauschning confessed to having yielded to the "fatally misleading, paradoxical illusion that [one had to] unite with a revolutionary element in order to attain the opposite of a revolution."

Rauschning was one of those ideological conservatives who eventually saw the errors of his ways. Whereas the left, notably the communist left, has been and continues to be severely censured for its erroneous reading of and policy toward rising fascism, on the whole the traditional right has been exempt from this criticism. Indeed, it is fashionable to say that the history of fascism is the history of its underestimation and misunderstanding, compounded by chance, error, and accident. But only reactionaries, conservatives, and centrists, certainly not militant socialists and communists, are given the benefit of this exonerative explication.

In any case, this explicative scheme of innocent misjudgment focuses too narrowly on visible individuals and their decisions, to the almost total neglect of the general context of class, power, and politics within which they acted. Even the most cursory examination of this over-all context reveals the full extent to which reactionaries and conservatives actually furthered the fascist cause before, finally, developing pangs of conscience. To be sure, the mixture of conscious, intended, and expedient complicity changed according to place, time, and political conjuncture. But that there was complicity is no longer open to question.

Even after he recanted, Rauschning nostalgically stressed the radical nature of pristine fascism, confessed that fascism's counterrevolutionary project originally had fired his zeal, and still hankered for a counterrevolutionary transformation, on condition that it be implemented without undue excesses.

Not too surprisingly, Western scholars, intellectuals, and ideologists paid no attention to Rauschning's counterrevolutionary professions. They preferred to seize upon two other themes in his analysis: that because fascism totally rejected "any sort of doctrine" it was a revolution of nihilism, and that because of its authoritarian political system fascism had great affinities with communism. These twin themes were incorporated into the West's ideological armory following the end of World War II.

It was then that, on the diplomatic level, the Grand Alliance broke up and, domestically, the left-oriented political truce expired in America, Britain, and other victor nations of the Western world. Almost overnight the international civil war was resumed. The euphemism "Cold War" was contrived to dissemble the real nature of this conflict which, though curbed during most of the Second World War, dated back to 1917. Ever since then, and most particularly in its acute phases, this universal confrontation required and generated an intense ideological duel. This being so, in the nascent Cold War both Washington and Moscow urgently required updated and sharpened ideational weapons with which to intervene in the internal affairs of third countries. The international civil war forced each side to intervene to strengthen embattled governments favorable to itself; to undermine, possibly overthrow, governments hostile to itself; or to bring about a shift to inert neutralism by heretofore firmly aligned governments.

Of course, intervention affected not only the foreign policy of third nations. It also impinged on their domestic life, though the sequence of change differed according to local circumstances. As for the means and methods of this international civil war, the major powers preferred to rely on instruments of control other than outright military force which, as always in international politics, remained the *ultima ratio.*

Among these instruments of control, ideology was of paramount importance in the political struggles of postwar Europe. In the liberated as well as defeated nations—Germany excepted —there was a groundswell of support for all parties of change, including the communist parties. Toughened in the crucible of the wartime resistance, their leaders resolved to capitalize on the explosive dislocations that were not of their making: chronic grievances and suspicions intensified by the pressing legacy of wartime suffering, privation, and promises of a new dawn. Even England experienced this groundswell, although she was spared the martyrdom of occupation and was deprived of the leavening of internal resistance: the Labor party was determined to build that country "fit for heroes" that had been promised in 1918, only to be travestied.

Between 1945 and 1956 both Washington and Moscow intervened in the internal politics of third countries, not least because the opposing sides in these countries asked, if not begged,
them to do so. The United States and its agents, some of them
self-appointed, supported governments, parties, factions, and
media that resisted the eruption of the forces of change, notably
of their most militant vanguards. Concurrently Soviet Russia
and its agents, some of them also self-appointed, encouraged
and assisted this eruption. Obviously, neither Washington nor
Moscow followed a consistent and undeviating course at all times
and in all countries. The interventionist policies of both were
particularly cautious in countries in which the other major
power claimed a primary security interest and therefore was
likely to respond with hot rather than cold war. In addition,
these policies changed in response to domestic developments
within the United States and the U.S.S.R. and fluctuated with
the changing geographic priorities of the worldwide confrontation of Washington and Moscow. But whatever these changes
and fluctuations, this much remained constant: Washington
never intentionally fostered revolution any more than Moscow
intentionally fostered counterrevolution. In sum, there were distinct outer limits to the flexibility, expediency, and opportunism
of the politics and diplomacy of competitive intervention.
The Soviet government, as well as Europe's communist and
fellow-traveling parties, entered the Cold War with a decisive
psychological advantage and a considerable ideological head-
start. Psychologically, they benefited from the remarkable performance of the Red Army on the battlefields and of communist
militants in resistance and guerrilla movements. Their status and
élan also gained from the fact that, notwithstanding grave tactical and theoretical errors, on the whole the communist view of
fascism turned out to have been more accurate than any other.
Admittedly, it was not until a year and a half after the Nazi
takeover in Germany that the communists switched from denouncing social democrats for being social fascists to summon-
ing them to a united or popular front against fascism. But this
failure to close ranks in time was far from unique with the
communists. Moreover, they realized their error and changed

course much more rapidly than others. To be sure, they had good reasons to do so: German communists and the East European rimland, which was Soviet Russia's security belt, became Hitler's prime target for attack. However, in retrospect the steep blood price they paid for their mistakes and survival overshadowed the naked self-interest that had motivated their abrupt doctrinal and practical reversal.

By comparison with this communist opposition to fascism, in the immediate postwar years the long-delayed, halting, and essentially unsuccessful reactionary and conservative resistance to fascism went nearly unnoticed, particularly in the lower and middle reaches of society. Throughout occupied Europe this resistance did not really show itself until the defeat of fascism, both national and international, seemed certain. By then it was too late to erase the harsh realities and memories of intended reactionary and conservative collaborationism during fascism's finest hours. These realities and memories were so intense that they momentarily obliterated those of the Nazi-Soviet pact and the concomitant "neutralism" of the communist parties from 1939 to 1941. And whenever they were reminded of their own diabolic collaborationism, the Soviets and communists discomfited their critics with the charge that Allied appeasement of Franco, Mussolini, and Hitler, which culminated in Munich, had left them no other alternative.

Of course, the political strategy of branding all anti-communists, including social democrats, fascists had a doctrinal basis. The communists never really jettisoned the thesis that fascism was nothing but a thinly disguised conspiracy masterminded by a fatally besieged capitalist class. In their perception this class was bent on making a desperate last stand that could only be both short and unsuccessful. They assumed that fascism was no more than a pliable instrument in the hands of the capitalist class, and that its ineffectiveness would become apparent in no time. Particularly once the depression dealt what communists predicted and hoped would be fatal blows to the capitalist world, they scorned rather than feared salvage operations whose early failure they anticipated and were poised to exploit.

But the communists had no monopoly on these and other

misinterpretations and miscalculations. As indicated above, reactionaries and conservatives had their own instrumental view of fascism. Moreover, they, too, were confident that even if fascists should succeed in grabbing power for themselves, their reign would be short-lived: lack of administrative experience and skills would compel fascists to defer to their politically seasoned reactionary and conservative partners once the forces of change were thoroughly routed.

As for the social democrats and leftist liberals, most of them were at least as apprehensive of a communist as of a conservative succession to fascism, which they, too, saw in instrumental terms.

With due allowance for notable exceptions, in very general terms it can be said that reactionaries and conservatives not only miscalculated but also cunningly used and loyally collaborated with fascism until, finally, they broke with it. On the other hand, again with notable exceptions, communists did not persist in their error and at no point deliberately collaborated with fascism, though independently they fished in the same troubled waters until mid-1934. Certainly in the immediate postwar perspective these two complicities seemed of an altogether different order. The complicity of the communists, such as it was, tended to be condoned, if not forgiven, because of the vital role they and their Soviet mentors subsequently played in the defeat of fascism. Also, their penance, in the form of their blood sacrifice, was not only on an infinitely larger scale than that of the reactionaries and conservatives, it was also less overdue and elitist, and therefore full of resonance for the social and political carriers of postwar renovation.

Meanwhile, the march on Rome in 1922, the Bulgarian coup in 1923, and the Nazi takeover in 1933 stimulated communist theorists to examine and interpret the fascist counterrevolution, to fit it into their doctrinal scheme. To be sure, they made and perpetuated consequential mistakes. In addition to the previously noted stress on the instrumental character of fascism, there was a stubborn blindness concerning the authenticity and scope of its social roots, the effectiveness of its programmatic and ideological "demagogy," and the centrality and efficacy of its paramilitarism. From first to last, communists ignored the mass psychology, charismatic leadership, and integral terror of fascism. Also, in their analysis of the manipulators of the fascist instrument, communist theorists, along with most others, failed to distinguish scrupulously between reactionaries, conservatives, and counterrevolutionaries.

But along with these defects and blindspots, there were trenchant and lasting insights. Precisely because they never had any doubts about the counterrevolutionary essence of fascism, communist analysts instantly saw it not in narrow, national terms but in the same broad, universal perspective in which they saw their own project. In addition, even though they overstated the instrumental nature of fascism, they steadfastly maintained that it could not break into power without the indulgence, encouragement, and cooperation of incumbent elites and institutions. They kept insisting on the movement's multiple roots in the existing class, social, economic, and political structure.

Whereas their diagnosis of the politics of counterrevolution remained shockingly primitive, communist theorists developed ever more careful profiles of the social carriers of fascism. Without ever slighting the importance of national and conjunctural factors, they differentiated between rural, small-town, and urban supporters. Some of these were said to rally because they were pauperized, others because they felt déclassé. Also, rather than see the peasants as a bloc, they separated tenant farmers from small and middle farmers who own and operate their property. As for the workers, they were declared immune, except for certain agricultural, domestic, and unemployed laborers. In the last analysis, however, communists saw the petty bourgeoisie and the new middle classes, provincial but especially urban, as the principal reservoir of mass support for fascism.

Once they understood that fascism was carried forward by such diverse clienteles, including disillusioned and unemployed intellectuals, communist observers began to concede the rationale and efficacy of fascist "demagogy." They noted that each of the major publics was mobilized with ideological and programmatic appeals specifically formulated and styled for its consumption. Fascists were said to take special care not to offend potential

converts or, in particular, essential patrons, paymasters, or partners. The one theme that communist spokesmen identified as
being central to fascist propaganda all over was not anti-Semitism—witness Italy, Finland, and Japan—but self-flattering and
expansionist nationalism.

Indeed, the communists never tired of warning that fascism
inevitably carried the seeds of general war: unable to solve
explosive economic, social, and political problems at home,
sooner or later fascist regimes would be forced to have recourse
to diversionary war, as foreshadowed in their stridently chauvin-
ist creeds.

No one will ever deny that the Soviets, the communists, and
their fellow travelers, in their evolving assessment of and policy
toward fascism, made grave theoretical and operative errors,
not to say blunders. But preoccupation with the reasons and
motives for these errors should not preclude attention to what
was accurate and useful in the communist diagnosis. And yet,
this is precisely what happened after World War Two. Western
scholars and ideologists became obsessed with the vituperative
excesses of the communist campaign against social fascists, as if
it had been the sole or prime cause for the Nazi breakthrough.
They reproved the rank expediency of the Nazi-Soviet pact, as
if it had not been a concomitant of the prior Munich agreement,
and they dwelt upon the commandeered disloyalty of Allied
communists from 1939–41, as if revolutionaries could be expected
at all times to put nation ahead of party. Rather than examine
these misdeeds contextually, Western analysts portrayed them
as typical of authoritarian regimes and parties that are fiend-
ishly unscrupulous in their pursuit of unlimited power and
dominion.

This was the beginning of a gradual shift from concern with
the causes and origins of fascism to concern with the structure
and operation of totalitarian systems, whether fascist or com·
munist. To the extent that Westerners continued the probe into
the rise of fascism they did so with multi-factor analysis that
was intended as a critique of the allegedly single-factor analysis
—i.e., class analysis—of the communists. In their scheme fascism
emerged as the product of an infinite variety of conjunctural

circumstances, social carriers, and political accomplices. And as a matter of principle they refused to rank the various factors in any order of importance.

Accordingly, economic dislocations and political deadlocks were said to be equally decisive precipitants and determinants of crisis; workers as susceptible to fascist appeals as peasants and the middle classes; social reformist themes as central to the fascist creed as anticommunist and jingoist slogans; communist and syndicalist converts to fascism as consequential accomplices as industrial, agrarian, and bureaucratic patrons. Needless to say, to refrain from assessing the relative importance of causal factors even of particular turning points is not only to renounce the responsibilities of meaningful historical explanation but also to evade the issue of whether fascism had a discernible revolutionary or counterrevolutionary thrust. *yes*

The thesis that fascism was a revolution of nihilism both symbolized and served this evasion. It shifted attention to the intellectual, cultural, and psychological aspects of fascism, away from the political, economic, and social anvil on which crisis politics is forged. This shift in emphasis coincided with the new preoccupation with the practice and consequences, rather than causes, of fascism.

It was at this point that Rauschning's canard about the identity of fascism and communism received scholarly and intellectual sanction. Scholars and action intellectuals ignored their own strictures against examining complex historical phenomena with preformed and hierarchically ordered organizing principles as they proceeded to formulate a concept of totalitarianism that could subsume both fascism and communism. In their monochromatic scheme, revolutionaries and counterrevolutionaries became totalitarians bent on subjecting first their own countries and then the world to a permanent system of oppression, exploitation, and dehumanization.

To be sure, Western intellectuals continued to debate whether totalitarianism was historically unique, or whether it was merely the latest version or admixture of older forms of tyranny, despotism, or dictatorship. But except for this dissonance, they reached general agreement on a definitional concept of totalitarianism as

totalitarianism

legally unrestrained government, dominated by a power-seeking charismatic leader whose instruments for total control of polity, society, and psyche include a single mass party, a rigid ideology, pseudo elections, systematic terror, state monopoly of mass communications, and a centrally directed industrial economy.

The exponents of this concept of totalitarianism stressed that the authority systems of fascism and communism were fundamentally identical, both of them being characterized by the same syndrome of institutional structures and processes. Totalitarianism soon came to be perceived and portrayed as standing in stark contrast and hostility to Western parliamentarism. Whereas during the Second World War the Nazi regime had been the principal embodiment of totalitarianism, now, in the Cold War, the Soviet regime became its chief incarnation. Quite imperceptibly, and perhaps also unintentionally, the theorists of totalitarianism smoothed and fostered the transmutation of wartime antifascism into postwar anticommunism.

The concept of totalitarianism was essentially static, in that it narrowly focused on the structures and operations of political authority systems. At best there was a passing concern with the causes and origins, the social and economic functions, and the historical development of the systems in question.

By excluding these diachronic dimensions from their typological and analogic analysis, the theorists of totalitarianism glossed over key substructural differences between communism and fascism. In fact, in their overreaction against the Marxist fixation on the socioeconomic bases and consequences of politics, they tended to ignore these altogether. There was nothing in their construct to suggest that the mainsprings of communism and fascism could be drastically different, possibly opposite.

It was not until the Cold War subsided in Europe and its front line moved to the Third World that the concept of totalitarianism began to be questioned. By then it was apparent that, unlike the major fascist regimes, the Soviet regime never depended on external war and conquest for internal political stability and survival. Even in its most extreme Stalinist phase, it fought the international civil war—notably in Greece, Italy, France, and also China—with great, some even say excessive, caution. The question arose as to whether this circumspection in international politics, so contrary to fascist foreign policy behavior, was conditioned by the nature and dynamics of Soviet Russia's internal system. The relatively calm transition to post-Stalinism gave still greater poignancy to this question, in addition to suggesting that perhaps charismatic leadership was less essential to the rise and maintenance of the communist than the fascist regime. (Neither Lenin nor Stalin was a rabble-rouser, though Lenin was an effective public speaker.)

Moreover, in the Third World the mainsprings and purposes of both revolution and containment were too immediately alive to be ignored. Developments in Cuba, Vietnam, and Indonesia legitimized and promoted the reintegration of the temporal, causal, and purposive dimensions into the perception and study of contemporary events.

In any case, the origins and functions of the communist and fascist regimes were anything but similar. To begin with, the Russian Bolsheviks were a relatively small party of organized militants who, capitalizing on the prostration of their country, struck and seized power from below. Admittedly, exasperated and war-weary soldiers, peasants, and workers, some of them previously politicized, rushed to their support. But these were not in the nature of a drilled mass or paramilitary movement recruited from dislocated segments of modernized and atomized society. On the contrary, to the extent that Russian society became atomized this was a consequence of the forced-draft modernization that followed rather than preceded the change in the authority system.

Secondly, the Bolsheviks first seized and then consolidated their power in opposition to consistently hostile economic, political, social, bureaucratic, and ecclesiastic elites at home and their supporters abroad. In short order, they permanently dislodged these elites through expropriation, expulsion, persecution, and terror. Some institutions, notably private property, religion, and the judiciary were changed beyond recognition. Others, such as the state bureaucracy, the armed services, and the diplomatic corps continued after a thorough change of top personnel.

Thirdly, an entirely new elite of propertyless politicians and experts surfaced to formulate and implement a revolutionary project for the basic transformation, including industrialization, of Russia. This elite was sworn to a comprehensive doctrine which not only fixed long-term social and economic goals but also defined the limits of day-to-day compromises. In sum, the revolutionary regime and project had an irreversible core. This was also the case in the satellite countries, where regime and project could neither have triumphed nor survived without Soviet Russian intervention.

Italian and German fascists took an entirely different road to power and, once in power, implemented an altogether different project. These differences in origins and development point to some elements that can legitimately be designated counterrevolutionary.

Mussolini and Hitler seized power from above. In fact, it may be more accurate to say that it was handed over to them. To be sure, before achieving this seizure or transfer, both leaders built controlled mass movements and regimented terror units. These were recruited in peacetime from the crisis strata—including ex-servicemen and frustrated nonproletarian youth—of developing or overdeveloped societies convulsed by recurrent and pressing economic as well as attendant political dislocations and contradictions.

The fascist movement did its best to heighten and embitter this crisis situation. At the same time, fascist leaders offered their shock troops as auxiliary forces of order to a panic-stricken ruling and power elite. Frightened by the specter as much as the reality of an impending communist revolution, this traditional though far from united elite not only closed ranks but also explored the terrain for an expedient alliance with the fascists. In the various stages of this exploration, and even before, important individuals and institutions of incumbent polity, economy, and society ignored, condoned, and eventually supported even the most naked fascist excesses.

In other words, both before and after they were in political control, fascists counted on the sanction and cooperation of the throne, the altar, and the sword. In both fascist Italy and Germany—in fact, wherever fascist or fascoid regimes were established—property relations remained unchanged. The industrial, commercial, and agricultural elites, though prohibited from continuing their separate and self-directing political activities, stayed in position, with their social and economic foundations intact. The same held true for the managerial, technocratic, bureaucratic, military, and ecclesiastic elites. Of course, a distinct fascist political class moved into a dominant position. But this new elite was not superincumbent, except in the spheres of politics and ideas. Rather, the fascist leaders mingled with the old upper strata which retained the superior social status, educational level, economic bases, and international contacts, and for which they had a convulsive mixture of contempt, envy, and, above all, need.

This comprehensive institutional, structural, and elite continuity—except in the encroaching political sphere—meant that severe and explosive dislocations and contradictions were temporarily defused and reduced, but not significantly eliminated. And when they threatened to erupt again, these deep-rooted distempers tended to be canalized into external belligerency and war. In both the internal and external phases of the search for stability and survival, the fascist regime's industrial-military complex played a key role.

Developments in China, Cuba, and Vietnam, as well as the Sino-Soviet tensions, have prompted Western scholars to concede that their concept of totalitarianism has been excessively static and rigid, failing to reckon with the above essential differences, in both origin and project, between communism and fascism.

In Europe, after 1944–1945, the containment of communism proceeded on two levels. The Western powers agreed on a geographic line beyond which the Soviet bloc would not be allowed to expand by direct armed force, should such ever have become its intention. The United States provided nearly all the determination, strategic design, high command, manpower, and resources for this vast military effort, concentrated in Europe.

This American-orchestrated military build-up also contributed, obliquely, to internal stabilization this side of the fortified line. It stimulated the self-confidence of governments and their supporters, pledged contingent internal security forces, and intimidated revolutionaries and their Soviet helpers.

But by far the most decisive aspect of America's contribution to domestic stabilization was the resolute injection of massive financial, economic, and ideological aid into both the victorious and defeated nations of Western and Central Europe. This nonmilitary intervention was calculated to undercut the internal sources of revolutionary ferment.

Throughout noncommunist Europe, except in Greece, this timely two-pronged intervention worked to perfection. Though weakened by war, the old economic, social, and ecclesiastic structures survived. They were sufficiently resilient to become girders for reconstruction, planned and implemented by political and managerial cadres of a reformist conservative bent. As a result, the over-all political thrust of European containment, both domestic and international, was restorative rather than reactionary or counterrevolutionary. A similar pattern unfolded even in prostrate Italy and Germany, where the reformist conservative *political* leadership and cadres first had to be reconstituted with Allied patronage and help. Because of its profound roots in the socioeconomic institutions and strata that had collaborated with fascism, this restoration stood in need of a historical sacrament, which instantly took the form of hyperbolic odes to the conservative and reactionary resistance to Mussolini and Hitler. Needless to say, this founding myth concealed that this resistance had been narrowly based, timorous, long-delayed, and essentially ineffective.

Compared to this restoration in Western Europe, including the Allied zones in Germany, the picture in Eastern Europe and the Soviet zone in Germany was altogether different. There Russia intervened, at first primarily with bayonets, to impose and enforce not a restoration but a revolution, also for security reasons.

Not that Western scholars and action intellectuals would have judged the Eastern European revolutions any less harshly if they had been truly indigenous. Certainly Western reactions to other communist revolutions since 1917 belie any such assertion. But the fact that communist regimes were forcibly superimposed on Eastern Europe enabled Westerners to attribute these revolutions entirely to the imperialist character and objectives of Stalin-ist totalitarianism. It seemed irrelevant that except in Czecho-slovakia and possibly eastern Germany, restorations in Eastern Europe most likely would have produced regimes that were undemocratic as well as anti-Soviet and anti-Russian.

In any case, the satellites were portrayed as mere extensions of the Russian revolution, which dated back to the First World War. After a quarter of a century the Allies found it easy to ignore the origins of that revolution. They also managed to maintain a discreet silence about their own intervention in the Russian Civil War, their own boycott and quarantine of Moscow, and their own appeasement of fascism, all of which contributed to the hardening of the Soviet system.

By the end of the Second World War, then, the historical question of why and how the communists triumphed and built their institutions had become largely academic and overshadowed by concern with the repressive workings of the Soviet system. At that very time, however, that same question about communism in China moved to the center of scholarly and ideological debate.

Even at the height of the Cold War in Europe, Stalin simply could not be charged with having coerced China into com-munism as he had Eastern Europe. Stalin had been far from con-stant and enthusiastic in his support of Mao Tse-tung, and the in-digenous nature of the Chinese communist revolution was too obvious to be seriously questioned.

Admittedly, war has been the great accelerator and intensifier of revolutionary conditions. Lenin capitalized on it in 1917, Stalin in 1944–45, and Mao as of 1931. And while war was the con-ditioner common to the advance of communism in Russia, East-ern Europe, and China, the party, guided by variants of the Marxist doctrine, was the chief instrument of mobilization, com-bat, and implementation.

But in the context of this discussion what matters is the dif-ferent place of civil war in the rise of communism in Russia and China respectively. In Russia, the civil war did not really start until after the seizure of power in November 1917, which was in the nature of a surprise coup. From their principal strongholds in and around Petrograd and Moscow the Bolsheviks then improvised an army in double-quick time. These emergency battalions, in which workers took pride of place, did not couple the revolutionary with the nationalist flag until foreign troops actively supported the Whites. Within less than four years the Bolsheviks were in control of the country which, though territorially truncated, was fully pacified.

In China the civil war was anterior rather than posterior to the final seizure of power and control of the mainland. It all began with the withdrawal of the communists to Kiangsi in the wake of their abortive coup in Canton in December 1927. Following the "long march" to the northwest, they built up an army of poor and middle peasants, not of workers. They rallied support with appeals of anti-imperialist nationalism and radical agrarian reform, the latter being implemented and displayed in those areas and provinces that came under their control. As "the soldiers became the fish and the people the water," the communists' guerrilla tactics became increasingly effective against the armies of the Kuomintang and Japan, both of whose troops were trained for positional rather than irregular partisan warfare.

In 1949, when they finally achieved full control of the mainland, Mao Tse-tung and his colleagues were in command of a vast peasant army and vanguard party. Even so, Communist China's "totalitarian" system was at best embryonic. Though there was the sectarian and factional in-fighting that is so characteristic of new revolutionary regimes, there was no evidence of bloody purges, either then or during the succeeding decade of consolidation. Perhaps this relative moderation was at least in part due to the absence of foreign military intervention and to the fact that because of Soviet aid the American-orchestrated quarantine remained ineffective.

At any rate, at the time it would have been difficult to use the concept of totalitarianism to convincingly equate Maoism with Stalinism (not to mention Hitlerism). Of course, Mao's drive into Korea in late 1950—comparable to Lenin's and Trotsky's foray into Poland in July 1920—came at the peak of the Cold War in Europe. It gave rise to the charge, therefore, that China and Russia were merely two parts of a single totalitarian monolith that was centrally integrated and controlled.

But this charge was exploded before it ever struck roots. It instantly became clear that even in the Korean crisis, Communist China never deviated from a cautious though vigilant foreign policy course. Presently, in 1953, Stalin's death precipitated and speeded the loosening of the Soviet Russian system and bloc. Three years later, in 1956, the abortive East European rebellions dramatized the hopes and limits of that loosening at the same time that they confirmed the West's recognition of Soviet Russia's security sphere in Europe. That same year, the Suez imbroglio—the swan song of nineteenth-century overseas colonial imperialism—demonstrated that England and France had no alternative: they had to acknowledge their own and Europe's subordinate military and diplomatic place in the new global system of international politics. They did so while the Cold War subsided in Europe, but developments in Indochina, North Africa, and Latin America served notice that the international civil war was on the upgrade throughout much of the Third World. There, many of the same conditions and forces that had fostered and characterized the rise of communism in China were increasingly in evidence.

Clearly, the concept of totalitarianism lacked the scholarly and ideological cutting edge for dealing with post-Stalinist Russia and her satellites, the independent development of Maoist China, the Sino-Soviet split, and the international civil war outside Europe. Another explicative scheme was needed, but one that would also continue to skirt the confrontation of revolution and counterrevolution.

By the mid-fifties American scholars and action intellectuals began to be preoccupied with problems of development and modernization in the Third World. Throughout noncommunist Europe—except in Greece—and in Japan the internal containment of communism proceeded in modernized or modernizing polities, societies, and economies. This being so, American intervention centered in countries whose structures were or could be geared for restorative projects of recovery and reconstruction. The governments and ruling classes that were the recipients of United States aid were able and ready, if not eager, to reduce the sources of internal instability and radicalism by combining economic growth with timely reforms. While fighting the international civil war on such favorable terrain, America never really faced up to the problems of effectuating containment in alliance with governments and elites that are determined to balk her strategy of fighting revolutions with reformist conservatism.

Significantly, in Europe this refusal was entered only by Greece and Spain (and Portugal), whose stages of development were more on the level of the Third World than of the Atlantic world and Japan. In both countries, however, the internal forces of revolution had been decisively defeated in civil war. Whereas in the case of Spain this outcome was achieved with the help of the Axis before the war, in Greece the Allies provided essential assistance after the war. Even though in both instances counter-revolutionary formations and methods were used to achieve victory, conservatives and reactionaries never lost their commanding places. They also shaped their post civil war regimes in their own image. With the revolutionary danger eradicated and awesome internal security forces in place, neither regime was about to press development and reform as a hedge against future dislocations.

Even so, Madrid and Athens became important links in the chain of containment—the *cordon sanitaire*—that was designed to check the revolution in Europe. They pressed for American aid to bolster up arrested polities, economies, and societies of distinctly rightist character. Washington answered their call; it even anticipated their summons. It did so in spite of clear-cut evidence that the receiver governments and oligarchies purposely painted all left oppositionists as communists so as to better justify putting repressive order ahead of reformist conservatism. Actually, successive American administrations willingly paid this price, insisting that both Spain and Greece were of prime strategic significance in the West's over-all military bulwark against world communism.

Similarly, Washington was not condemned to support governments throughout the Third World that it knew to be sworn to a status quo that violated all of America's libertarian and reformist professions. Rather, it chose to do so, especially because, in comparison with Spain and Greece, the prospects of revolutionary dislocations were considerably more real and imminent in these countries. In addition to outright military assistance, which once again fortified internal security forces, America provided technical, financial, and economic assistance to governments and elites that gave first priority to shoring up incumbent authority systems.

Especially, but not exclusively, because of intense population pressures, these regimes counted on this nonmilitary assistance less to improve economic and social conditions than to prevent their further disintegration. However reluctantly, Washington went along with this prophylactic strategy, for to withhold aid from retrograde regimes was to run the risk of fostering if not precipitating highly explosive political polarizations. In that event the logic of containment could easily force the United States to side with whatever civil and military forces promised to repress revolutionary forces, if need be by pre-emptive violence. Needless to say, American policy makers sought to avoid the kind of impasse that would leave them no alternative but to lay bare and shoulder the ultimate requirements and consequences of containment.

The Third World, then, became the new frontier not only for the theorists of the social sciences but also for the practitioners of containment. Even so, scholars and action intellectuals failed to concern themselves, systematically, with the taproots of situations that required containment. They also neglected the high costs—political, economic, and social—of continuing stagnation or of slow-gaited economic growth to underlying populations, and their disproportionate benefits to pre-existent elites, both parasitic and productive.

Instead of facing up to these less glorious and not so visible aspects of American supported or countenanced containment, Western intellectuals confined their attention to situations that were more congruent with Washington's world creed. Scholars and ideologists cooperated in the formulation and implementation of a concept of gradual modernization that precluded refractory disruption and violence. Their developmental model became both an analytic tool and a prescriptive injunction. It was also put forward as Western capitalism's alternative to the ongoing Soviet Russian and the unfolding Chinese communist modernization projects.

Whereas the concept of totalitarianism concealed the conservative and reactionary mainsprings of fascism, so this concept of gradual modernization neglected the matrix of class, status, and politics within which development is shaped. This matrix came to view only when gradualist projects suffered shipwreck. It took the breakdown of these projects to bring to light their conservative and reactionary social, economic, and political components, alliances, and mortgages. In Cuba, the Dominican Republic, and Vietnam, disruption bred civil strife; in several Latin American countries, Pakistan, and Indonesia it precipitated pre-emptive military coups of varying scope and intensity. And all these eruptions were caught up in the international civil war, now centered outside Europe. Incidentally, the military coup in Greece in 1967 merely corroborated that containment and intervention, as practiced and consummated in developed countries, were unsuitable for the developing nations.

In these developing nations Washington distinctly prefers to support center-left or centrist governments, confident that their developmental policies are the most effective antidote to potentially convulsive instability and disorder. But under the umbrella of this intervention, rightist civil and military forces feel themselves to be and are encouraged to conceive of themselves as essential backstops to law and order. The leaders of these forces are adept at misrepresenting loyal reformists as dangerous revolutionaries; at playing on the specter of communism, to which Washington is, of course, oversensitive; and at preparing pre-emptive coups with which to convert their very considerable yet abeyant influence and power into full authority.

Whether Washington secretly condones, supports, or even engineers such coups is less important than the fact that it never sequesters them, as it does revolutionary takeovers. To be sure, military takeovers never fail to evoke pious disavowals punctuated by the momentary suspension of normal diplomatic representation and foreign aid. But these are ritualized expressions of innocuous displeasure, calculated to attenuate the disfiguration of the image of libertarian containment. No sooner has the first shock worn off than Washington anoints the new power holders by resuming not only full diplomatic relations but also all forms of assistance.

Scholars and ideologists are not inclined to study and expose the repressive political and social costs of giving primacy to containment. Their writings are more likely to justify Washington's policy of calculated accommodation. They do so with the argument—implicit or explicit—that all authoritarian regimes, except outright revolutionary ones, can be trusted or are historically programmed to implement gradualist modernization, which they insist is the passkey to eventual democratization. Of course, tacitly they also deliver a homily that dictatorial regimes which embark on revolutionary rather than gradualist modernization cannot and do not create the preconditions for their own moderation or else do so at an intolerably slow pace.

Given these premises there are good reasons to ward off or reverse revolutionary takeovers. But whereas conservative and reactionary political or military forces, whatever their changing admixtures, tend to break into power from above, revolutionary movements must break in from below (except if they are placed in power by the bayonets of a conquering revolutionary army). In the event that a revolutionary movement, whether outlawed or not, organizes guerrilla units and secures operational bases, civil war becomes likely unless the government manages to crush the revolutionaries completely and swiftly. Such civil strife, when it does materialize, is an effect as well as a cause of unrelenting polarization, with both sides becoming increasingly authoritarian, violent, and uncompromising. By assisting the antirevolutionary side in local engagements of the international civil war, the United States becomes the indispensable auxiliary of political, social, and economic forces of reactionary, conservative, and counterrevolutionary bent.

First Cuba and then Vietnam demonstrated that every modernization project is forged in political, class, and social conflict that can become disruptive. Presently it became evident that such disruptions could not be fitted into the construct and prescription of gradual modernization within systems of "moving equilibria." Without seriously questioning or revising their most recent analytic and political concepts of modernization, scholars and action intellectuals simply proceeded to treat these ruptures separately, as if they were unrelated to the politics of modernization.

Moreover, rather than label these disruptions for what they are—namely, civil wars—social scientists once again enlisted a pseudo-neutral vocabulary-*cum*-concept to explain them. Almost overnight totalitarians of the extreme left and right became insurgents and counterinsurgents on opposing sides in "internal"— not civil—wars.   " internal war "

This latest terminological metastasis enabled action scholars to avoid not only differentiating but also choosing between revolution and counterrevolution. Most of them insisted that their precipitate interest in problems of internal wars was dispassionate and value-free. They made this claim in spite of the fact that the same government that subsidized much of their research became their client. In fact, few of these social scientists hesitated to advise successive American administrations on ways to improve intervention in support of the counterinsurgent side in internal wars. (Certainly none of them applied themselves to perfecting the methods of the opposing insurgent side!)

As happens so frequently, prescriptive social scientists and ideologists of the noncommunist left converged and reinforced each other. Admittedly, they expressed themselves in different idioms, but the substance of their advice and conviction was identical. Both scholars and ideologists urged that military operations be combined with vigorous socioeconomic reforms so as to make the counterinsurgent soldiers "the fish" and the people "the water." They sought to adapt the nonmilitary core of the revolutionary strategy to antirevolutionary purposes, in the hope of making the counterinsurgent cause more popular and less exclusively military. Scholars and ideologists alike hate to concede that civil wars inevitably pass through a polarizing phase that is equally brutalizing for both sides, and that in the last analysis the antagonists in civil wars do have diametrically opposed interests, values, and objectives.

The concepts of totalitarianism, gradual (equilibrated) modernization, and internal war, each in its own way, obstruct the examination and comprehension of some of the most important issues of contemporary history. In particular, they detract attention from the genesis, course, and nature of the confrontation of revolution and counterrevolution in the context of a global civil war.

How to account for this blind spot or distortion? The scholars and intellectuals who formulated and disseminated the ostensibly value-free concepts of totalitarianism, modernization, and internal war will deny that their vision was circumscribed by political and ideological factors, or by a craving for social, professional, and financial advancement. Provided they acknowledge that such influences and motives might have tacitly and unconsciously affected their thought, their denial will, of course, be accepted at face value. But whatever the admixture of objectivity and bias in their intellects, these three conceptual constructs served and still serve the needs of America's power elite and its world project.

This ruling class was hostile to any suggestion that the world crisis of the twentieth century be viewed and projected as a confrontation between revolution and counterrevolution. To begin with, except for brief intervals, as of 1917 communists appropriated this interpretation for themselves and propagated it with considerable success. Moscow, and later Peking, both inspired by Marx, insistently proclaimed that revolution and counterrevolution, and their constant interaction, were two sides of a single process rooted in the final breakdown of capitalism and of colonial imperialism. With this interpretation the communists proudly arrogated the entire revolutionary ground for themselves, while indiscriminately stigmatizing all their opponents as carriers of counterrevolution.

In an age of mass politics, counterrevolutionaries, conservatives, and reactionaries fight shy of having that role imputed to them. Quite apart from the obvious but intended oversimplification, they know that to be politically effective they need to project a popular, reformist, and emancipatory image of themselves and their various containment projects. Whereas counterrevolutionaries went about this with aggressive fervor, conservatives and reactionaries proceeded with greater reserve. But all alike were determined to conceal the stabilizing, coercive, and impounding features of their opposition to revolution.

Although America became the chief carrier of international containment, she was least disposed to assume an overt antirevolutionary posture. Such a stance would have distorted not only her external but especially her internal impulses. In addition, as indicated before, it would have clashed with her self-characterization as a nation born to a revolutionary tradition and mission. Even so, the political class and its advisers realized that it would be as futile to claim the revolutionary scepter for America as it would be to charge first Moscow and then Peking with being counterrevolutionary. In the broad context of the international civil war, even Soviet Russia's repressive intervention in Hungary in 1956 and in Czechoslovakia in 1968 could not make such an inversion plausible. Accordingly, American policy makers as well as scholars and ideologists were well advised not to make the confrontation of revolution and counterrevolution central to their perception and interpretation of the contemporary crisis.

One of the consequences of this unnecessary but serviceable myopia has been a stubborn aversion on the part of social and behavioral scientists, including historians, to the study of counterrevolution. In turn, this great scholarly and intellectual abnegation has had the effect of keeping the term and concept of counterrevolution safe for facile political rhetoric. The time has come to face up to the scholarly and political obligation to clarify the counterrevolutionary realities of contemporary history.

2. Some Preliminary Distinctions

Ever since 1789 the study of revolution has been pursued far more intensively and systematically than the study of counterrevolution. Eventually, specialists in the sociology, politics, and psychology of knowledge will want to explain the motives and causes for this disproportion in scholarly and intellectual concern. Meanwhile, it is beyond dispute that there exists a much more significant fund of empirical and conceptual knowledge about revolutions than about counterrevolutions.

One need only compare the voluminous and high-quality attention that has been lavished on the French Revolution with the sparing and mediocre treatment of its counterrevolutionary side. Quite properly, *La Contre-Révolution,* by Emmanuel Vingtrinier (1924–1925), and *La Contre-Révolution sous la révolution,* by Louis Madelin (1935), never achieved a prominent place in the impressive historiography of the French Revolution.

To be sure, the imbalance is beginning to be noticed and corrected. In recent years Jacques Godechot (1961) has provided a panoramic vista of the ideas and actions of the counterrevolution both before and after the fall of the Bastille; Paul Bois (1960) and Charles Tilly (1964) have examined its local taproots in the Vendée; Jean Vidalenc (1963) has provided a profile of its émigrés; and J. J. Oechslin (1960) has traced its political course after the Restoration. Even so, the counterrevolutionary "side" of the French Revolution still awaits its Labrousse, Mathiez, Cobban, and Soboul. Future scholars will have to wrestle, above all, with the causes, carriers, dynamics, and objectives of the aristocratic reaction, of the émigrés, of the early hostility from across France's borders, and of the white terror.

The imbalance is just as great in the study of the Russian Revolution. Central aspects of its counterrevolutionary half wait to be explored in depth. Specifically, historians will want to probe into the mainsprings of the "aristocratic reaction" from 1905–

1914, of the White side in the civil war, of the emigration, and of the intervention and containment from beyond Russia's borders.

It is not really surprising that Crane Brinton's *Anatomy of Revolution* (1938) was not matched or followed by an "anatomy of counterrevolution." When he set out to hypothesize recurring patterns in the English, American, French, and Russian revolutions, Brinton enjoyed a number of enviable advantages. To begin with, he himself was a seasoned specialist in the well-plowed history of the French Revolution. In addition, he was able to draw on a considerable accumulation of assimilated data about the other three revolutions; he was attuned to social scientists who were formulating heuristic concepts of revolution; and along with these social scientists, he was challenged by the raging Russian Revolution, which continued to shake the world about him.

Would-be students of comparative counterrevolution enjoyed none of these advantages. Until very recently they faced a relative empirical and conceptual wasteland. Moreover, the contemporary realities of fascism were not the stimulant to the scholarly examination of counterrevolution that those of communism were to the study of revolution. Whereas during its lifetime fascism aroused little sympathy in leading scholarly circles, after its defeat Western scholars centered their attention on its internal rather than contextual life.

But however formidable these handicaps may have been in the past, they are fast subsiding. Important spadework is under way on the counterrevolutionary side of the four major revolutions that were included in Brinton's triptych. Furthermore, now that the deficiencies of the concept of totalitarianism are becoming evident, the large fund of data about the nature and dynamics of fascism is about to be structured with the help of radically different organizing principles and new research designs. Just as revolutionary France has been and continues to be the historical laboratory for the refinement of heuristic concepts of revolution, this essay urges that fascist Italy and Germany, as well as fascoid developments in other countries, become the historical terrain for the exploration of heuristic concepts of counterrevolution.

When trying to clarify an important political phenomenon, it is customary to consult the classics for inspiration and guidance. In this instance, however, this time-honored procedure is not very rewarding. Aristotle never really distinguished between revolution and counterrevolution. In his schema, the origins and causes of constitutional overturns are viewed under three headings: the psychological motives of key actors, their purposes, and the precipitants of their actions. Aristotle repeatedly noted the fear of the loss of power, status, or wealth as a precipitant of preemptive political maneuvers. He also stressed the low social origins of tyrants who build their popular support by the manipulation of demagogic appeals. And last, Aristotle spoke of those circumstances under which rulers may find it expedient to "foster alarms . . . [and] make the remote come near" in order to get "a firmer grip on their constitution."[1]

Neither Machiavelli nor Bodin spoke to issues of revolution or counterrevolution, though, like Aristotle, both of them took account of the proclivity of governments to channel mounting internal conflicts into external tensions or war.[2]

In turning to the philosophes, Burke, the romantic conservatives, and the rational reactionaries, it is well to remember that they wrote, first and foremost, as *engagés* ideologists. Their political commitment is perhaps best illustrated by that often-cited exchange between two luminaries on opposing sides of the issue. Condorcet self-confidently proclaimed that "lorsqu'un pays recouvre sa liberté, lorsque cette révolution est décidée, mais non terminée, il existe nécessairement un grand nombre d'hommes qui cherchent à produire une révolution en sens contraire, une contre-révolution." Determined to claim the high ground of continuity and legitimacy, de Maistre angrily retorted: "Le rétablissement de la Monarchie, qu'on appelle contre-révolution, ne sera

---

[1] Ernest Barker (ed.), *The Politics of Aristotle* (Oxford: Clarendon, 1946), Book V, passim.

[2] Niccolò Machiavelli, *The Prince and the Discourses* (New York: Modern Library, 1940), p. 79, and *The Art of War* (Indianapolis: Library of Liberal Arts, 1965), pp. 40–41; Jean Bodin, *Six Books of the Commonwealth*, abridged and translated by M. J. Tooley (Oxford: Basil Blackwell), pp. 168–169.

point une révolution contraire, mais le contraire de la révolution."[3]

The books, pamphlets, articles, and speeches of these action intellectuals are an essential source for the study of the conflicting ideological and programmatic projects of the French revolutionary era. In addition, they eventually became a source of inspiration and provocation to the contestants in the era of the communist revolution.

Characteristically, the leaders and backers of the *Action Française* established a special chair at their political institute in honor of Rivarol for the specific purpose of making earlier counterrevolutionary ideas and insights relevant to their own enterprise. In 1906 Louis Dimier, the first incumbent of this sham academic chair, delivered a series of lectures on *Les Maîtres de la contre-révolution*.[4] Among these, in addition to Rivarol, he included Maistre, Bonald, Courier, Sainte-Beuve, Taine, Renan, and Veuillot.

Dimier sought to reduce Rivarol's politically inspired and Maistre's religiously founded critique of the French Revolution to a scientific and rational system to be used in contemporary political combat. In his judgment, intellectuals of his persuasion could take for granted a mounting popular revulsion toward the revolution's legacy. They could also trust the French public's profound attachment to the past and its unwavering devotion to the church. What was needed was an intellectualization of the counterrevolutionary position, less for the rank and file than for the leaders, both present and future. These had to be disabused of simplistic conspiratorial views of revolution. To be sure, Freemasons, Jews, sectarians, and criminals were the chief carriers of the corrosive revolutionary bacillus. But what mattered was that the contagion had spread so far and deep, notably among the attentive publics, that police operations alone could no longer fight the infection.

Instead, Dimier proposed to carry the battle into the intel-

---

[3] Antoine-Nicolas Condorcet, *Oeuvres,* vol. XII, p. 619; and Joseph de Maistre, *Considérations sur la France,* p. 164.
[4] Paris: Librairie des Saints-Pères et Nouvelle Librairie Nationale, 1907.

lectual and ideological arena. There he meant to fight the wrong ideas of the contemporary world with counterrevolutionary ideas and maxims grounded in the critique of his great precursors. He announced that the *Action Française* would disseminate the ideas of the great masters of counterrevolutionary thought; would teach and explain their doctrines to young intellectuals; and would extract from them precepts relevant to present conditions. On the whole, however, the masters of the counterrevolutionary tradition concentrated heavily on what to them were the execrable methods, excessive costs, and disastrous consequences of revolution.

Marx and Engels, of course, fixed their attention on the causes and kinetics of revolutionary surges, breakthroughs, and abortions. Even so, they fully realized that the success or failure of any revolution was in no small measure a function of the policies pursued by antirevolutionary forces. Both attached capital importance to the shifting alliances within the antirevolutionary triad of conservatism, reaction, and counterrevolution. As contemporary observers of the revolutionary developments of 1847–1852 and of 1870–1871, Marx and Engels concluded that the greater the push for the extension of political into social revolution, the greater the cooperation and cohesion among the antirevolutionary factions.

In 1848, in the aftermath of the June days in Paris, the big bourgeoisie "growled" less against those above them as they increasingly "trembled" before those beneath them. In Berlin, for example, Ludolf Camphausen and the big bourgeoisie eventually closed ranks with the "feudal, absolutist counterrevolution." But because Camphausen had left the crown, the bureaucracy, and the army essentially intact, this turn to the right made the bourgeoisie the political prisoner of the "counterrevolutionary camarilla." As Marx put it, "Camphausen sowed reaction in the interest of the big bourgeoisie but harvested it in the interest of the feudal party, of the aristocracy, and of absolutism."

Clearly, Marx spoke suggestively to the politics of counterrevolution. To begin with, he insisted that it was quite as internationally linked as the politics of revolution: "In Italy, in Naples, the European counterrevolution struck its first blow; in

Paris—the June days—it assumed a European character; Vienna was the first reverberation of the June counterrevolution; and in Berlin it was both completed and compromised."

Secondly, Marx was fully sensitive to the fierce struggle for political primacy within the expanding antirevolutionary camp. More particularly, he saw that in the face of mounting social pressures, those who controlled the bureaucracy and the army acquired a special advantage. Indeed, it was because of their solid foothold in these two institutions that in most places beleaguered preindustrial strata and elites secured a disproportionately large degree of effective influence and power.

Third, for Marx the consequences of counterrevolution were essentially political. Constitutions were recast, and so were the powers and roles of *political* classes. But what Marx considered the infrastructures of politics remained essentially unaffected. Not that such political changes were altogether without economic, social, and even cultural repercussions. But these did not significantly alter the basic foundations of society and polity. In 1848–1849, the fear of popular forces inclined the bourgeoisie to yield most of the political power it had captured so precariously. It retreated in the wake of military repression, followed by varying combinations of ultraconservative, reactionary, and counterrevolutionary political rule. In France alone the republic survived, tenuously. But soon Napoleon III stepped forth to capitalize on renewed fear of radicalism and on governmental deadlock to supplant the political rule of the bourgeoisie with methods—and for purposes—that foreshadowed fascist projects of later days. But as Marx noted, throughout the continent the bourgeoisie, together with the other possessing classes, came through the crisis and constitutional realignments with their material and social power substantially unscathed.

In other words, the social and economic interests of the bourgeoisie were protected. Moreover, even though its political pretensions and influence were curbed, they were not reduced to nothing. Rather, instead of governments systematically favoring the unfettered capitalist modernization to which the bourgeoisie was sworn, they now either tolerated or tamed it.

Meanwhile, the army and the police, commanded by officers

rooted in the crisis strata, played a vital role in repression, stabilization, and consolidation. Eventually Engels warned against premature revolutionary risings, insisting that in peacetime these officers and their civilian associates made incumbent authority systems impregnable, the more so because their troops were loyal and their modern equipment devastating.

Still, it must be said that Marx and Engels did not distinguish, systematically, between conservatives, reactionaries, and counterrevolutionaries. They failed to methodically differentiate the socioeconomic roots of these factions; their political objectives, styles, and methods; and their ties to incumbent political, military, and ecclesiastic institutions. Along the way Marx and Engels indiscriminately referred to the *leaders* of the opposition to revolution as conservatives, reactionaries, and counterrevolutionaries. They also attributed to all of them an essentially reactive behavior and denounced rather than explicated those of their actions that were offensive and preemptive in nature.

But whereas Marx and Engels were excessively vague about the economic and psychopolitical moorings of conservative, reactionary, and counterrevolutionary leaders, they were considerably more incisive about the class and status background of their following. Over and over they stressed that the political carriers of opposition to revolution came from the economically and socially uprooted strata of the major classes. Class as such was not decisive, but rather the extent to which segments of different classes experienced or were apprehensive about *déclassement, defunctionalization, or alienation.* With their fears and anxieties heightened by crisis conditions, segments of the nobility, bourgeoisie, urban *petite bourgeoisie,* landowning peasantry, and workers contributed to a pool of potential antirevolutionary energy and support. Marx and Engels never really discussed how the fears of these crisis strata were manipulated for political purposes. Nor did they take an interest in the identity of the manipulators; in the nature and structure of the resulting political movements; or in the correlation of class and status with degrees of power and activism within these movements.

On the other hand, Marx was particularly precocious in his sensitivity to the central importance of the *petite bourgeoisie,* in the large cities especially but also in the provincial towns. Both he and Engels considered this stratum to be the critical swing group in revolutionary situations. It was caught between the bourgeoisie above and the proletariat below. Whereas the class and status positions of both of these strata were dependent on the modernizing sectors of the capitalist economy, that of the intermediate *petite bourgeoisie* was tied up with the survival of obsolescent forms and methods of production. In this precarious condition, it was torn between hatred of large-scale capitalism, whose efficiency cut into its economic livelihood, and fear of the proletariat, which threatened its petty material and social privileges.

Still, according to Marx and Engels, this interstitial stratum had little autonomous staying power, particularly in times of crisis. In an early phase of crisis it may have joined the workers in an assault on the greater bourgeoisie. But the moment the capitalist system, which it needed to survive, was itself endangered, the *petite bourgeoisie* recoiled from this expediential alliance and placed itself in the service of restabilizing leaders. In the Marxist perspective, the *petite bourgeoisie* ultimately preferred gradual erosion by advancing industrial capitalism to sudden supersedure by the revolutionary proletariat. In the crunch, therefore, this "dangerous class," or "social scum," was bound to play the part of a "bribed tool of reactionary intrigue."

Recent studies of mass movements and mass politics have refined rather than overturned the Marxist analysis of the class and status composition of the political carriers of opposition to revolution.[5] But whereas Marx and Engels, however defectively and scantily, situated these social strata in concrete political contexts, later social and behavioral scientists have tended to altogether neglect doing so. Specifically, they have missed the ultimate interconnection of these insecure and vulnerable social layers with the superordinate cartel of anxiety.

In any case, only very few social and behavioral scientists have faced the counterrevolutionary phenomenon head on. And

---

[5] E.g., see Emil Lederer, *State of the Masses* (New York: Norton, 1940), and William Kornhauser, *The Politics of Mass Society* (Glencoe, Ill.: The Free Press, 1959).

the few who have grappled with it were inspired to do so by the turmoil which consumed Central and Eastern Europe after the First World War. Particularly in Weimar Germany—this century's principal and eventually most infernal battleground of revolution and counterrevolution—social scientists groped for a concept of revolution that could also accommodate the counter-revolutionary dimensions and propensities of acute crisis situations.

Whatever their politics, German social scientists had to come to terms with the salient differences between Germany's revolution from above in 1918–1919 and Russia's revolution from below in 1917–1920. In addition, they had to take account of the Frei-korps and the nascent National Socialist movement; the "liberation" of Munich; the abortive Kapp and Hitler *Putsches;* the rash of political assassinations; and the calculated obstruction of the new order from within the corporate economy, bureaucracy, judiciary, army, church, and university.

These antirevolutionary organizations, events, and actions were paralleled throughout most of neighboring East Central Europe. Hungary—and, with less excess, the four new Baltic countries—experienced the full force of this counterthrust: the overthrow of Bela Kun's regime was followed by a fierce white terror in the guise of anti-Semitic pogroms. German social scientists simply could not overlook these and similar developments, including the rise of fascism in Italy. Besides, such émigré scholars as Oskar Jászi, Karl Mannheim, and Aurel Kolnai were among them to make sure that antirevolutionary repression not be lost sight of.[6]

At any rate, once sociologists proceeded to wrestle with the concept of revolution, four different views of the relationship of revolution and counterrevolution claimed attention. According to the first view, revolution inevitably provokes a reaction from those opposed to it. From this mechanistic perspective, the resist-

---

[6] Jászi, *Magyariens Schuld, Ungarns Sühne: Revolution und Gegen-revolution in Ungarn* (Munich: Verlag für Kulturpolitik, 1923); Mann-heim, *Ideologie und Utopie* (Bonn: F. Cohen, 1929); Kolnai, "Gegenrevolution," in *Kölner Vierteljahrshefte für Soziologie,* vol. X, nos. 1–2 (1931–1932), pp. 171–99, 295–319.

ance to revolution is organized by recently ousted civil and military elites, as well as by disenchanted revolutionaries who break with the newly established regime and orthodoxy.[7] The former in particular enlist external support for their military campaign, the ultimate objective of which is the restoration of the *ancien régime*.[8] In this scheme, then, the counterrevolutionary drive consists of whatever forces, either singly or in coalition, either with or without foreign aid, oppose the consolidation of a fundamentally changed authority and social system; and this drive has a self-evident impulse in favor of a return to conditions approximating the *status quo ante*.

The premise underlying the second position regarding the relationship between revolution and counterrevolution is that revolutionary conflict and change are qualitatively different from conflict and change under conditions of equilibrium. Pitrim Sorokin lived "in the circle of the Russian Revolution" before writing *The Sociology of Revolution* as an exile in Czechoslovakia. By then he stressed that "'reaction' was not a phenomenon beyond the limits of revolution but . . . an unavoidable part of the revolutionary process itself, its second half."[9]

This same premise braces the formulations of Leopold von Wiese and Theodor Geiger. Von Wiese defined "revolution in the public weal as a sudden and quick reallocation of power." It was likely to be marked by coups and counterrevolutionary obstructions, both of which he considered "social processes" essentially similar to revolution.[10] Geiger pushed this holistic conception a few steps further.

Revolution is the abrupt and complete changeover of social structures and systems. However, revolution consists not only of destructive

---

[7] Stefan Szende, *Europäische Revolution* (Zurich: Europa Verlag, 1945), pp. 72, 75.

[8] Lyford P. Edwards, *The Natural History of Revolution* (Chicago: University of Chicago Press, 1927), pp. 119–21. Incidentally, Edwards' "biological" model of revolution was taken over by Brinton in his *Anatomy of Revolution*.

[9] *The Sociology of Revolution* (Philadelphia: Lippincott, 1925), pp. 3, 7.

[10] Von Wiese, in *Verhandlungen des III. deustchen Soziologentages*, Jena, September 1922 (Tübingen: Mohr, 1923), p. 13.

acts but also of acts of innovating construction. Accordingly, revolution tends to be a process of longer duration which may be punctuated by one or more mass explosions. In the same way other violent acts may accompany it: revolts, coups, putsches, and the like. As discrete acts these can be rooted in the revolution. In this sense counterrevolution is part of revolution. Not that it is a revolution. Rather, counterrevolution belongs to it, results from it in the form of a refluent movement. It is literally a *re-action*.[11]

But Geiger, like Sorokin and von Wiese, stopped short of identifying those special characteristics which set counterrevolution apart from the other violent paroxysms of the revolutionary process. Also, in his perception, the vector of counterrevolution was purely reactive and its objectives indeterminate.

(3)   Without breaking out of the reactive mold, the third conception focuses on the nature of the counterrevolution itself. In order to successfully parry the blows of a revolutionary assault, counterrevolutionary leaders are said to find themselves compelled to adopt a project that is the inverse of the revolution. As if by reflex the counterrevolution borrows its central ideas, objectives, styles, and methods from the revolution; and its own ferocity develops in proportion to the revolution's excesses.[12] Although mimetic, the counterrevolution acquires a project and thrust that transcend the mere restoration of order and of the *status quo ante*.[13]

(4)   In the fourth scheme revolution and counterrevolution are nearly indistinguishable. Both are said to be illustrative of a seamless process of revolutionary change, the Vendée and peasant *jacqueries* being variants of the same general genus and process as the French, Russian, and Chinese revolutions. Most important, this schema for the study of discontinuous change contains guidelines for causal analysis. In the latter, attention

---

[11] Geiger, *Die Masse und Ihre Aktion* (Stuttgart: Enke, 1926), p. 59.
[12] This is an example of Gabriel Tarde's notion of "imitation par opposition." Cf. Karl Mannheim, *Essays on Sociology and Social Psychology* (New York: Oxford, 1953), p. 89, n. 1.
[13] Cf. André Découflé, *Sociologie des Révolutions* (Paris: Presses Universitaires, 1968), pp. 121–22.

is rigorously centered on the "multiple dysfunctions" unsettling social systems; the degree of elite intransigence in the face of heightened pressures for instant, radical change; the accelerators and precipitants of crisis conditions; and the reliability of military and police forces in the event of insurrection.[14]

But among social scientists, Aurel Kolnai stands out for having explored the problem of counterrevolution as such. He was the only one to insist that counterrevolution, though symbiotically intertwined with revolution, has a discrete existence and momentum of its own. In his analytic framework Kolnai accords primary attention to the complicity of conservatives and reactionaries with counterrevolutionaries. At the same time he stresses the intramural rivalries within this triad before, during, and after the seizure of political power.[15]

Even so, Kolnai's over-all perspective is that of the other social scientists, including historians, who consider acute multiple dislocations, cleavages, and contradictions as symptoms and causes of *prerevolutionary* situations. The question arises whether such conditions could not just as validly be viewed as producing and constituting a pre*counter*revolutionary situation. Obviously, revolution and counterrevolution are two inseparable sides of one and the same refractory historical constellation. But more often than not, incumbent elites and institutions successfully control or crush convulsive disruptions. Whatever its internal dynamics, elite intransigence is far more likely to produce effective repression from above than to provoke successful insurrection from below. Even in extreme situations, public authorities, through the police and the army, maintain a near-monopoly on the legitimate use of violence. This gives them immeasurable advantages in the timing and tactics of prevention, containment, and punishment of any insurgents they may seek to curb.

In any case, crisis situations have a double-edged nature and impulse. Excessive preoccupation with their revolutionary aspects

---

[14] Chalmers Johnson, *Revolution and the Social System,* Hoover Institution Studies: 3 (Stanford University, 1964); and Johnson, *Revolutionary Change* (Boston: Little, Brown, 1966).

[15] Kolnai, "Gegenrevolution," in *Kölner Vierteljahrshefte für Soziologie,* vol. X, nos. 1–2 (1931–1932), pp. 295–98.

has contributed to the relative neglect of their equally essential and dialectically linked counterrevolutionary facets.

Because of their symbiotic relations, counterrevolution and revolution cannot be understood and examined in isolation from each other. Any effort to bring greater conceptual clarity to the study of counterrevolution requires, at a minimum, a prior though tentative conceptual definition of revolution.

It was Metternich who distinguished three types of revolution: palace revolutions against individuals, political revolutions against forms of government, and social revolutions against the bases of society. As for Marx he was interested in the interpenetration of the political and social factors in the revolutionary situation and process. He insisted that every revolution is political insofar as it overthrows the existing authority system, and social insofar as it breaks up the existing socioeconomic system.

Be that as it may, revolution is not similar to palace revolt, military coup, urban riot or insurrection, bread march, or general strike. Of course, any one or any combination of these can become a tributary precipitant, accelerator, or decelerator of an unfolding revolutionary project, thereby affecting its shape and direction. Similarly, revolutionaries ought not to be confused with advanced reformers, anarchists, or primitive rebels. To be sure, at critical moments, by design or chance, the latter's actions can converge to produce the vector of forces needed to bring down an incumbent authority system. Before long, however, these elements of change fall out among themselves over the implementation and further extension of this breakthrough. (Incidentally, historians never cease to be fascinated by the internal workings of this sequential convergence and decomposition of revolutionary coalitions. Depending on their political persuasions or affinities, historians censure, commend, or exonerate the leaders of the principal factions for the direction and timing of their partisan maneuvers.)

What, then, is a revolution? It is a violent, fundamental, and abrupt change of incumbent elites, status and class relations, institutions, values, symbols, and myths. This radical change is initiated and implemented by militant political actors sworn to a nurtured and internally coherent doctrine of innovation and

— see also Schurmann

not of cyclic recurrence. The revolutionary ideology guides the formulation of concrete programs, restricts the scope for compromise and opportunism, and sets limits to the inconsistencies of appeals that are designed to make converts and to neutralize opponents.

A revolution has one additional characteristic: the governments and peoples of other nations, near and far, simply cannot remain indifferent to paroxysmal ruptures and innovations whose doctrinal sources and project have an ecumenical character. The nation that is the subject and carrier of revolution becomes a prototype for emulation. It also becomes a center for the diffusion of ideas, programs, and policies to the four corners of the world. On the one hand, foreign governments and their supporters, sometimes goaded by émigrés, resolve to contain, tame, or destroy this cradle of fermentation and contagion. On the other hand, inspired and sometimes assisted or guided by leaders in the vanguard base, the philorevolutionary opposition to these governments proceeds to emulate and exploit the other nation's revolution for its own purposes.

As to counterrevolution, it is not the same as the control or repression by incumbent governments of street demonstrations, strikes, local insurrections, or mutinies. Nor are counterevolutionaries to be confused with reactionaries and conservatives, although the affinities and connections between these components of the antirevolutionary triad are decisive in all aspects of the counterrevolutionary enterprise.

Reactionary political actors are unabashed and pretentious critics of existing society. They reject the world about them for being decayed, corrupt, pernicious, and repugnant. Consumed by an all-pervading pessimism about the present and future, they distrust all agents and carriers of innovation. Reactionaries tend to be suspicious, if not outrightly hostile to science, technology, education, industry, and urbanization, and also to youth, intellectuals, and experts. Their hostility seems motivated by a combination of guilt, hate, and mistrust that is nourished by the fear that their and their children's life chances are condemned to continuing deterioration if history stays on its present course. This being so, they want the direction of history changed, if necessary by force. Reactionaries advocate a return to a mythical and romanticized past. In this past they seek the recovery and restoration of institutions—monarchy, church, landed estates, communities—which sustain a hierarchical order of privileges and prerogatives and which also form a rampart against the corrosive leveling of polity, society, and culture. Once recovered, these good old days would be frozen, perpetually.

Reactionary political actors propose to lead a retreat back into a world both lost and regretted. At the same time that they epigrammatically idealize this past, in order to stimulate political action in the present they denounce all their antagonists as devious conspirators sworn to the corruption of contemporary man and society. This conspiratorial view enables reactionary leaders and their followers to ignore the economic and social causes for the erosion of their own expendable stations in life. It also conceals, even from themselves, the large degree to which their own privileged continuance in the blighted present depends on calculated political log-rolling within the cartel of anxiety, in which conservatives and counterrevolutionaries are their partners.

In relatively normal times, reactionaries tend toward self-isolation. This posture is bolstered by their disdain of conservatives who accept and support the status quo, and their repugnance toward counterrevolutionaries who cater to the masses. But as soon as clouds of instability and unrest gather, they master their antipathies in order to collaborate more closely with their partners in fear. At a minimum, reactionaries want order maintained or restored against rebels or revolutionaries, the known present being preferable to the uncertain future, even if only marginally. Beyond this, they stand prepared to capitalize on the conjunctural crisis and the recourse to violence in order to reclaim part of their lost paradise or to reinforce the political pillars necessary to uphold their superannuated economic and social position.

As for conservatives and conservatism, they defy conceptual characterization at least as much as any other major segment of the political spectrum. In particular, their clarification tends to be hindered by stereotypical common wisdom. At almost all times the motives, conduct, and purposes of conservative political actors are said to be the "sensible" correlates of mature age, of temperamental or psychological equipoise, or of vested interest— or of a combination of these generational, personality, and positional factors. Certainly, in ordinary times, conservative political actors are satisfied and identify with the status quo. They also meet demands and pressures for purposive yet gradual change flexibly and pragmatically.

But how do conservatives react to actual or imminent disruptive change? In turbulent times the "good sense" of middle-aged, psychologically balanced, and institutionally secure individuals is severely tested. When confronted with rising social dangers, conservatives are challenged to assign priorities among their multiple purposes; to organize their influence and power for deliberate political action; to set the terms and limits of collaboration with kindred yet rival political elements; and to shape strategies and tactics suitable to the situation. This reassessment and self-definition, which are accompanied by severe intra-elite struggles, require and generate ideological and programmatic formulas which, in times of normalcy, are foreign to conservatives and conservatism.

Indeed, equilibrium and consensus preclude self-conscious and ideological conservatism, whereas times that are out of joint precipitate and foster it. More specifically, systematized rather than natural conservatism develops in response to social groups and political factions that foment and exploit disorders with the help of systematized political formulas of their own.

Conservative thought is in the nature of an articulated refutation, not of a creative innovation. It is designed to give coherence to the defense of traditional social, economic, and political institutions and of traditional aesthetics, morals, and manners.

Quite clearly, not only generational, psychological, and positional categories obscure the dynamics of conservatism, but categories of an essentially philosophic nature do so as well. Conservatives and conservatism react to specific historical conjunctures, notably to acutely unsettling ones. In such disruptive situations, potential group or class support for conservatism points in different directions, as does the ideological and programmatic response.

Mannheim quite rightly stressed the connection between the prospects of social groups in crisis situations and the style, form, and content of the ideas of which they become carriers. In his scheme, "the key to the understanding of changes in ideas is to be found in the changing social background, mainly in the fate of the social groups or classes which are the 'carriers' of these styles of thought." Perhaps Mannheim's conception is excessively one-sided. He tends to place all the stress on the impact on ideas of infrastructural changes, leaving insufficient room for reciprocal and interacting relations between them.

At any rate, in times of crisis the social carriers of conservatism separate into roughly three major groups: those attaching primary importance to maintaining their position, those seizing this opportunity to improve their position, and those seeking to minimize and slow down the deterioration of their position. Although all three are beneficiaries of the existing order, there are important differences between them.

Old possessing classes with secure status are likely to give first priority to maintaining their position, to be defensive in outlook, and to envisage moderate reform as one of the antidotes to a revolutionary challenge. Social groups that have substantial but recently acquired stakes that give them only superficial status are more prone to become aggressive in the defense of their new positions and to seize any opportunity to advance still further. Then there are those groups whose material stakes and rewards are modest. Some of these have time-honored status; others, whose stake was acquired only recently, aspire to attain this fixed and coveted status. But both have little and are afraid of winding up with still less. As a consequence they become as predisposed to offensive action in defense of their worlds as those of new wealth and status become in the protection of theirs.

The question arises as to when and how these three relatively distinct social groups influence the formulation of various conservative prescriptions. The political leaders of the three factions use and shape these prescriptions in their effort to galvanize social carriers to support their respective projects. They also need them to hammer out the purposive and strategic platform on which, in case of need, they will make a common stand. In and of itself conservatism is not creative. It postulates no theory, no system, and no long-range plans. It is without ultimate ideals against which to measure daily performance. Its essence lies in its praxis, whose content and method change with circumstances. In other words, in conservatism practice is ahead of theory, the concrete ahead of the abstract, the specific ahead of the general, and historical reality ahead of distant utopia.

Even so, there are kernels of theory and principle whose intellectualization bolsters and directs this praxis. Most of these are in the nature of negations or rebuttals of the principal tenets of opposing ideologies. But they are no less important for being reactive and not initiatory.

A pessimistic view of man is at the core of the conservative world view. Man is said to be weak, irrational, self-seeking, and sinful. Human nature being cast for all time, men can never hope to devise laws, education, and precepts capable of improving the individual. At best society, which has precedence over man and is morally superior to him, strives and manages to tame his worst instincts and impulses. It does so by subjecting him to a complex network of roles, norms, customs, traditions, beliefs, rituals, and prejudices. All these social relations and arrangements are organically interlocked as well as divinely and historically consecrated. To change or rearrange any one of these pillars is to endanger the entire edifice, thereby risking the neglect of essential human needs and the eruption of dormant human passions.

Men are also unequal physically, intellectually, and characterologically, and cannot be equalized or leveled by decree. While man's congenital inequality makes stratification natural and necessary, his innate depravity requires political authority, both social and political subordination being girded by ideologies of deference and resignation. Differential rights and duties are defined and arbitrated by ruling elites which, whatever their educational level, are rooted in and have respect for private property. To the extent that there is personal freedom, it is contingent on this private property and attendant preservative inheritance laws.

This longed-for stability and order is achieved by the encouragement of countervailing forces. At the same time that they sustain pluralism, these forces contrive to produce an equilibrium. This self-regulating process is lubricated by the reconciliation of differences through continuing compromise.

As noted above, in times of crisis conservatives are challenged to articulate and defend the values, institutions, and practices of existing societies which, in ordinary times, they take for granted. The greater the intensity and extent of this challenge, the more deliberate and explicit the conservative reaffirmation. If this challenge becomes ideological as well, the conservative reaffirmation is likely to also assume that character.

The degree to which conservatism becomes ideological also depends on the relationship of forces among the three major segments of its social carriers. It would appear that the greater the actual and potential force of those strata that are insecure in wealth, status, and power, the greater the likelihood that conservatism will become doctrinal, ideational, and dogmatic. In that event, the creed that emerges is one of feeling and mood rather than of thought and program. It takes the form of a reification, celebration, and inflammation of life forces, spiritual virtues, communitarian values, and national glories. These professions of self-flattery and nostalgia tend to be paired with sharp assaults on negative reference groups, both at home and abroad.

In many respects this ideological conservatism concurs with reaction and counterrevolution. There are significant family resemblances among all three in terms of social carriers, ideas, attitudes, and objectives. Indeed, in times of acute crisis conservatives, reactionaries, and counterrevolutionaries look to this common social, ideological, and psychological terrain to provide the foundations for political collaboration among themselves.

It is important, therefore, to stress rather than to underplay their philosophic convergences and interconnections; their conflation in the minds of overlapping audiences; and their contribution to an atmosphere favorable to the politics of resentment, fear, and anxiety.

Whether of obstructionist or reformist temperament, in ordinary times natural as well as pragmatic conservatives are effective in the defense of the status quo. But once a serious challenge arises they tend to lose their effectiveness and self-confidence. This is not to say that these conservatives abnegate or yield their political, social, and economic influence and power. When the politics of compromise and accommodation run aground, conservatives look for other and more effective procedures. One alternative is to join the ideological conservatives, reactionaries, or counterrevolutionaries; another and more likely option is to collaborate, either tacitly or openly, with one or more of these three associated groups.

In other words, under conditions of heightening dislocations, contradictions, and cleavages the praxis of pragmatic, nonideological conservatism becomes chimerical. Conservative political actors, parties, and their clienteles, faced with the destabilization of the system which they themselves are unable to prevent or arrest, do not vacate their seats of influence and power. Rather than leave the road open to radical reformers or revolutionaries, they hold the ring either for their repression before they seize power or for their overthrow after they have done so. In the process, they sanction policies and methods that inevitably exceed the politics of either preservation or restoration. Indeed, in order to contain or crush forces that strike at the foundations of their polity, society, and economy, conservatives ally themselves with reactionaries and counterrevolutionaries who, in their own but less radical ways, also repudiate the legitimacy of the existing order.

Conservatives decide to travel this road in spite of their strong distaste for and quarrels with the ideas, style, methods, and ultimate objectives of their partners. Under assault they jettison their flexible position, best summarized in Metternich's credo that "la stabilité n'est pas l'immobilité." They now incline to work with a cartel of anxiety that gives precedence to order over freedom, stability over change, and preventive over retributive repression. Conservative leaders assume this hardened posture

at a time when many of their habitually deferential and re-
signed followers become increasingly consumed by doubts and
uncertainties. The swelling ranks of skeptics and the disaffected
crave reassurances that are not so much rationally convincing as
emotionally satisfying and stirring. Pragmatic conservatives have
neither the formulas, nor the talent, nor the taste to meet this
requirement. Compared to them, reactionary and counterrevolutionary leaders are both ready and eager to play on the distempers and expectations of large segments of the political and
social clientele that in ordinary times support the conservative
bastions of the establishment. Counterrevolutionary leaders especially combine this zest for metapolitics with a resolve and
strategy for offensive action. Although conservatives realize
that this militancy violates their operational canon, they condone
and, if need be, support it as the *ultima ratio*.

In sum, in ordinary times conservatives can afford to be purely
practical and empirical in defense of the established order, while
claiming special credit for being antidoctrinaire and above partisan politics. In times of crisis, however, the logic of their position forces them into joining, condoning, or supporting those
advocating an antirevolutionary prophylaxis that is both ideological and aggressive.

part two

Framework

3. Counterrevolution: A Heuristic Concept

Like revolution, counterrevolution feeds on socioeconomic dislocations, discontents, and cleavages. These are intrinsic to industrialization, urbanization, and demographic change under market-economy conditions. Defeat in war and breakdown in economy merely increase the intensity, accelerate the tempo, and expand the scope of pre-existent tensions that ultimately stem from class, status, and power incongruities. If these tensions are not to become disruptive, notably when heightened by cataclysmic contingencies, they require political mediation.

But mounting infrastructural strains sap the effectiveness of political regulators even in countries that have tested constitutional traditions, effective channels for interest articulation, and operative political institutions. In addition, especially in the contemporary era, crisis conditions produce party leaders who systematically foster and organize the political fallout of economic, social, and psychological distress at the same time that they deliberately obstruct the machinery of political conciliation.

Admittedly, both revolutionary and counterrevolutionary leaders adopt this twofold political strategy. By so doing they cut into the support of the moderate and flexible center to the advantage of their respective camps, both of which are equally unyielding. One of the consequences of this polarization is the further paralysis of the politics of negotiation and compromise at the precise moment when group demands become urgent as well as conflicting and explosive. Faced with this mounting danger of disruption, incumbent governments readily yield to pressures for giving greater scope to individuals and agencies charged with the enforcement of law and order. Significantly, the advocates, directors, and yeomen of coercion have strong affinities

59

for and ties to those segments of the crisis strata that become the social carriers and political accomplices of the counter-revolution. In other words, the intensity and direction of any counterrevolutionary thrust are reciprocally related to this convergence of the forces and politics of order with the forces and politics of anxiety.

A reservoir of counterrevolutionary energy is located in many different segments of economy, society, and polity. There are potential recruits among tenant, small, and middle farmers; artisans, craftsmen, and shopkeepers; white-collar employees, professionals, and civil servants; rural, domestic, and occasional laborers; job-, income-, and status-seeking degree holders. Even in normal times these intermediate strata, which are insecure in both income and status, harbor latent resentments, fears, and anxieties, and in times of crisis these feelings are exacerbated. Even more important, they are activated by counterrevolutionary leaders who are eager to harness them for their own purposes.

Counterrevolutionary leaders have none of the prestige of traditional ruling classes and strategic elites; they share none of their bases of economic and social influence and power; and they have none of their fixed political clienteles. Instead, they start *de novo*: by mobilizing and regimenting superannuated, unhinged, and inert individuals and groups, counterrevolutionary leaders build the basis of power that enables them to become a new but claimant *political* counterelite.

This political counterelite is not recruited by social privilege or inheritance. The social origins of counterrevolutionary leaders prepare them for their self-given assignment of mass mobilization and articulation. More likely than not they have family, geographic, status, professional, and economic roots in the poor gentry, *petite bourgeoisie,* or new middle classes. This background sensitizes them to the distempers, interests, and aspirations of the composite crisis strata from which they draw their following.

Similarly, this political elite is not recruited according to pre-existent criteria of knowledge, skill, and achievement. Instead, these criteria are defined in response to the functional needs of changing conditions. Some counterrevolutionary leaders are skilled in the manipulation of signs, symbols, and rhetoric; others in political organization and administration; still others in paramilitary drill and assault.

But whatever their social background and their functional skills, counterrevolutionary leaders specialize in mobilizing the crisis strata by inflaming and manipulating their resentment of those above them, their fear of those below them, and their estrangement from the real world about them. Though the members of this nascent political elite may themselves be driven, individually and collectively, by multiple anxieties and irrational motives, they tend to be rationally methodical in the exploitation of the psychic discomforts of others.

Reactionary and conservative leaders are inclined to remain locked into the politics of deference and accommodation. Particularly in times of uncertainty they lack the self-confidence, disposition, and know-how to bid for the support of crisis strata, whose members they consider vulgar, fickle, and dangerous. Counterrevolutionary leaders, for their part, contemptuously reject deferential politics in considerable measure because it is beyond the reach of relatively low-born leaders such as themselves. While berating the practitioners of politics-as-usual for being effete and self-serving, counterrevolutionary leaders champion and engage in mass politics. In fact, they revel in it.

Their self-given assignment consists of aggregating the composite crisis strata into a unified political movement. Before it ever becomes the chief cornerstone of counterrevolutionary power, this aggregation serves incumbent government and society, first, by stemming the rush into the revolutionary camp and, second, by priming a critical mass to actively resist or repress revolutionary uprisings. Particularly in urban centers and provincial towns, counterrevolutionary leaders perform a critical and timely function: they give a sense of direction to crisis strata which, given additional time and distress, might well consent, psychologically, to their degradation and decline, and then look for redress to the revolutionary movement.

Just as the standards for admission to the counterrevolutionary elite are improvised in accordance with functional needs, this same functional improvisation characterizes the formulation of

counterrevolutionary appeals. These are designed, if not contrived, to incite and galvanize the crisis strata to political action.

But these appeals are not derived from a pre-existent doctrine
or ideology. To the extent that any one or combination of these
ever takes a coherent and systematic shape, it does so after the
fact. Counterrevolution is essentially a praxis. Its political doctrine is in the nature of a rationalization and justification of prior
actions. It is a pseudo doctrine.

Admittedly, this doctrine is given an ideological cast. But
even that is calculated and instrumental. As of the 1870s it became increasingly clear that to be effective, the struggle against
Socialism required a distinct popular ideology. According to
some, this ideology is in the nature of an invention; according
to others, it is a rediscovery of an earlier doctrinal dispensation.

But whether invention or rediscovery, or an admixture of the
two, the counterrevolutionary ideology is inconsistent. And so
is the counterrevolutionary program. This inconsistency is not
really surprising, given the uses to which ideology and program
are to be put. Both are needed to mobilize and maintain mass
support among highly diversified crisis strata; to entice and
reassure conservative and reactionary partners; and to lure interested patrons.

The creation of a mass basis has first priority, since without
it, or without the demonstration that they can build one, counterrevolutionary leaders remain political nonentities. The style
as well as the substance of their appeals is prescribed by the
nature of the adherents they propose to rally.

The potential for popular support is greatest among disaffected, resentful, anxious, frustrated, and impassive individuals,
interests, and groups. Rather than allay their fears and appre-
hensions, the spokesmen of counterrevolution foster and play
on them. Not that they fail to make concrete remedial proposals.
But to the extent that they do, the socioeconomic heterogeneity
of their prospective followers, allies, and paymasters dictates
programmatic vagueness, incoherence, and flexibility. In turn,
this programmatic amorphousness is muffled by soaring rhetoric
and incessant sloganeering, both of which are meant to fire

debasing and ultimately vindictive, brutal, and aggressive emotions.

In fact, one of the chief earmarks of counterrevolutionary ideology is that it exalts passion to the near paralysis of man's reasoning faculties and potentials. More particularly, it extols those individual passions which can feed collective paranoia and aggressiveness. The presumption is clearly against either cooling base passions or transmuting them into the sort that can become not only ennobling but also supportive of rational reflection and learning. It is almost as if, in pursuit of a compliant mass following, counterrevolutionary leaders seek to animate and reinforce "the inhuman, the brute," which, according to Hegel, "consists in being guided only by feelings and being able to communicate only through feelings."

In the last analysis, the counterrevolutionary project is far more militant in rhetoric, style, and conduct than in political, social, and economic substance. In the former respects, it can be likened to the revolutionary project. To be sure, its spokesmen mercilessly and savagely denounce all aspects of contemporary life, institutions, and culture. They also claim to have the blueprint and resolve for an instant and permanently stable and secure millennium. But both this sweeping denunciation of the present and this cryptic design for the future are revolutionary more in appearance than in reality.

Although they excel in exposing and overstating the cracks in a crisis-torn society, counterrevolutionary leaders do not account for them in any coherent and systematic way. They are not intellectuals, or intellectuals in politics, who are inspired or fanaticized by any great theoretical text, either past or present. Rather, they are self-taught empiricists and improvisers who have recourse to whatever ideas may serve their purposes, and in the process they convert or reduce these ideas to striking and phantasmic phrases.

In addition, counterrevolutionary leaders lack the education and temperament for rigorous theoretical diagnosis and prescription. But even assuming this is not so, or assuming they are surrounded by theoretically sophisticated advisers, politically they cannot afford the internal consistency that distinguishes a body of interrelated analytic and remedial principles from capricious demagogy. Counterrevolutionary leaders are so positioned that they need to revile incumbent elites and institutions without foreclosing cooperation with them. Similarly, they mean to inflame the frustrations and speak to the socioeconomic demands of their popular clienteles without turning them into sworn and ungovernable rebels against the establishment.

Accordingly counterrevolutionary leaders accuse the ruling class and its coactive strategic elites less of causing than of conniving with and benefiting from the corruption, exploitation, disorder, and disaggregation of existing society. Though incumbent elites smart under this charge, their pain is assuaged by the general ideological profession in which the denunciation is lodged. In times of crescive turmoil, perturbed conservatives and reactionaries approve or even endorse the counterrevolutionaries' rampant broadsides against science, technology, industry, capitalist competition, urbanization, and cosmopolitanism. This protest against progressing modernism is combined with vituperative attacks on political equality, party politics, and free expression, which growing segments of the old elite and their supporters also want curbed in times of serious crisis.

Whereas the attack on free political institutions includes an explicit summons for the adoption of a popularly ratified dictatorial authority system, the assault on economic and social institutions is not tied to any specific or radical cure. There is thundering but equivocal talk of reform, relief, and subsidies favoring the urban as well as rural crisis strata, interspersed with equally vague calls for confiscatory taxation of excess profits and for regulation of big industry, commerce, and agriculture.

These are strikingly mild injunctions, the more so in comparison with those of revolutionaries and advanced reformists. Certainly capitalists are not insensitive to this contrast. In addition, the counterrevolutionary platform means to have government underwrite the survival of economically besieged individuals, interests, and regions. Particularly in times of depression, the supporters and leaders of reaction and conservatism also urgently require political props to shore up their perilous economic position. As a result, while the leaders of relatively efficient, competitive, and self-confident economic and social forces at first merely condone the counterrevolutionary project as the lesser of two evils, those speaking for forces whose chronic insecurity is suddenly intensified instantly tend to collaborate with it.

Of course, all would-be coalition partners, paymasters, and government sponsors, no matter how conservative or reactionary, have a low tolerance for radical economic and social reforms. It is in this knowledge that counterrevolutionary leaders make or authorize essentially specious reformist pronouncements which are calculated to energize the lower and middle strata without excessively frightening or offending the upper ones. And in any case, in their propaganda they place greater stress on profound changes in attitude, spirit, and outlook than in economic and social structures. Whereas the masses are the primary target of this propaganda, its central themes are drawn from the reactionary *cum* conservative decalogue.

The counterrevolutionary clarion call is for order, hierarchy, authority, discipline, obedience, tradition, loyalty, courage, sacrifice, and nationalism. In other words, the appeals for psychic conversion, regeneration, and preparedness are fashioned out of traditional as well as familiar ideas, symbols, and myths. Their doctrinal foundations, which are less manifest, are also those of conservatism and reaction: a pessimistic view of human nature; the derogation of reason and rationality; the negation of equality; the precedence of community over the individual; the suspicion of novelty and innovation; and a Hobbesian conception of the international environment.

But there is one ingredient that is essential and peculiar to the counterrevolutionary formula: combining the glorification of traditional attitudes and behavior patterns with the charge that these are being corrupted, subverted, and defiled by conspiratorial agents and influences. Moreover, this charge, which reactionaries rather than conservatives are inclined to endorse, also includes a clarion call for ritualistic purification.

It is another earmark of the counterrevolutionary propagandist that he foments popular hatred and wrath against conspiring groups and individuals whose nefarious and insidious machinations are said to be aided from abroad. This Trojan horse is stigmatized and arraigned for masterminding, if not executing, the corrosion and ruin of government, society, and culture.

Such a conspiratorial rather than critical-analytic view of history serves any number of purposes: it provides semieducated publics with an uncomplicated, coherent, and plausible explanation of an otherwise confusing crisis; it enables the members of the crisis strata to explain away their own superannuation, inadequacy, and powerlessness; it helps humiliated individuals to salvage their self-esteem by attributing their predicament to a plot; and it furnishes overwrought persons and groups with proximate, tangible targets on which to vent their frustrations and hatreds. In addition, the conspiratorial "explanation" shifts the onus for the crisis from would-be conservative and reactionary partners to powerless and expendable minorities.

All in all, ideology and program are operationalistic and functional: counterrevolutionary leaders shape them into an instrument of political mobilization as part of their project for physical control of the state apparatus. The doctrinal sources of this ideational weapon are conservative, archaic, and atavistic; its substance and structure syncretistic, contrived, and incoherent; its presentational form and style rhetorical, facile, and histrionic; its intended audiences semi-educated, victimized, riled, and bitter. The counterrevolutionary project has a brazenly negative thrust. While its critique and disvaluation of existing polity and society are comprehensive and effective, its constructive purposes remain deliberately inchoate and equivocal. To the extent that there are professions of consequential socioeconomic reform, these tend to become muted once the breakthrough into power either appears feasible or is consummated, or both.

In contrast with their revolutionary opposites, then, counterrevolutionary leaders have an altogether more expedient and instrumental conception of ideology and program. Whereas a revolution can be conceived as a coherent idea and utopian vision that have found bayonets, a counterrevolution is in the nature of bayonets in search of a fabricated idea and a millenar-

essence is here:

violence + ideals — relationship between

(얼민주의)

ian charge. It is this salience of bayonets that contributes to the high priority of organization, discipline, drill, and violence in the counterrevolutionary project.

Even though so many of the appeals of counterrevolution are suffused with archaisms, they are disseminated by skilled experts in modern communications. These make systematic use of the latest media, even when staging mass festivals and rallies whose pageantry and liturgy are distinctly reminiscent of other times. Yellow journalism, radio, and cinema help to make occasions of local pomp and circumstance into larger, energizing occasions in which themes of nostalgic local and regional communitarianism commingle with affirmations of indomitable national unity, consecration, and will.

Resolved to bypass, swamp, and eventually castrate parliament, counterrevolutionaries become specialists in the politics of the streets and piazzas. It is from the public thoroughfares that they mean to apply pressure on all branches of government with an explosive yet controlled mixture of voice and violence; of psychic and physical action; of mind and brawn.

The drillmasters among them organize and train paramilitary formations. These have a multiplicity of purposes: to impress embattled crisis strata with the combative readiness and élan of the movement that beckons them; to wreak individual and collective terror in order to intimidate and neutralize opponents, as well as in order to weave blood ties among activists; to serve as a praetorian guard for studiedly conspicuous leaders and rallies; and to proffer standby or supplementary striking forces to interested private associations and public agencies.

Counterrevolutionary assaults, raids, and punitive expeditions tend to be provocative and aggressive. They are executed by men whose social background, psychological set, and ideological creed precondition them for recourse to brute force. This bent to violence gives them a decided advantage over those they attack. Even the most *enragés* revolutionaries are distinctly less martial in persuasion and therefore at a disadvantage in head-on street encounters. But there are other reasons for the expert success of the forays executed by the paramilitary arm of the counterrevolutionary movement: the large number of ex-military men, notably noncommissioned and low-ranking officers, among the shock troops; the relative military unpreparedness of those they attack; and the neutrality, passive or active, of the local police and constabulary.

Brazen paramilitary demonstrations and pitched street battles exacerbate rather than dampen the climate of insecurity, suspicion, and intemperance that is so central to the double-edged juncture—to the prerevolutionary *cum* precounterrevolutionary crisis. Characteristically, the supreme leader adopts a purposely and transparently ambiguous position. On the one hand, he claims that the forays are spontaneous outbursts of popular fury, beyond his control, against subversive revolutionaries. On the other hand, he applauds the shock troops for the efficiency and courage with which they take repressive measures that the incumbent authority system allegedly fails or is hesitant to take.

In other words, at the same time that the political leaders of the counterrevolutionary movement unleash and abet the politics of the street that compounds disorder and unrest, they commend themselves as sterling champions of law and order. They contend that they alone can curb their own ultras, that they alone can provide a backstop to regular security forces, and that they alone can muster mass support for the containment and repression of revolutionaries.

This, then, is the critical point at which counterrevolutionary leaders make the connection between the politics of anxiety, and movement from below, and that of order from above. They know that the ruling and possessing classes, including their subservient strategic elites, become uncertain, bewildered, and impressionable in the face of mounting chaos and disorder. Accordingly, the claimant counterelite brandishes the specter of explosive revolution, all the time exaggerating the immanence, ubiquity, and striking power of this revolution and its agents.

And, indeed, the fear of real or, more likely, imagined revolutionary eruptions inclines most conservatives and reactionaries to consider cooperation with the leaders of the counterrevolution. These cooperative relations develop gradually and under the impact of changing conditions: at different times some silently condone, others covertly encourage, and still others publicly en-

dorse and support counterrevolutionary measures that are bla-
tantly aggressive and violent.

Needless to say, conservatives and reactionaries abhor the ver-
bal, behavioral, and organizational style and excesses of their
new-found counterrevolutionary partners. But whatever the differences in method and pace, these fade into unimportance next
to the first priority on which all three, under some circumstances, are agreed: to prevent, crush, or overthrow the revolution. Not that these three components of the antirevolutionary
triad ever become fused or stop jockeying for position between
and among each other. Their cooperation remains strictly expedient. Whereas the upper cartel of anxiety needs the services
of proven masters of mass and paramilitary mobilization and organization, counterrevolutionaries need patrons who will furnish
them with a mantle of legitimacy, with political leverage, and
with funds.

Conservatives and reactionaries are confident that the risks of
cooperation are minimal. They expect counterrevolutionary leaders to remain dutiful auxiliaries, no matter how brash their pretensions. In any case, they assume that their coadjutors are dis-
qualified from first place by their low social status, limited
education, financial dependence, administrative inexperience, and
doctrinal incoherence. Counterrevolutionaries, for their part, rely
on conservatives and reactionaries to provide them with the
time, space, and resources to build an impregnable and awe-
inspiring bastion of autonomous political power. All through
their makeshift cooperation, the leaders of each of the three factions keep their respective larger purposes in view: the reactionaries to turn back the clock of history; the conservatives to
firmly reoccupy their multiple seats of power; and the counterrevolutionaries to seize control of state and government for themselves.

While it is important to identify and examine these social and
economic roots of the mass support and of the internal leadership of counterrevolutionary movements, by itself this kind of
social and prosopographical inquest—no matter how complete and
accurate—is very misleading. Because, after all, the development
and success of any counterrevolutionary movement is totally con-

tingent upon the changing attitudes and policies of incumbent ruling classes, elites, and institutions. These, in turn, are affected by the changing preferences of their own supporters, as expressed through organized interest, pressure, and political groups.

There is need, therefore, for careful attention to the wider political and class context and structure within which any counterrevolutionary movement develops and functions. Under crisis conditions, leading members of the upper classes, both within government and outside, give first priority to the protection and preservation of their threatened positions and possessions, if need be by collaboration with counterrevolutionaries. The spokesmen and officials of those classes and status groups that rely on government subsidies, patronage, and preferment for their privileged survival tend to be the first to veer in that direction. It is this upper cartel of anxiety, stagnation, and insecurity, intermittently joined and prodded by leaders of normally self-confident and secure sectors of economy and society, that urge varying degrees of sympathy, connivance, complicity, and collaboration with the counterrevolutionary movement.

Those advocating and engineering this collaborationism are peculiarly susceptible to the fear of the specter of revolution, which counterrevolutionaries manipulate so adroitly. Objectively the danger of revolution and the threat to the upper strata may never reach critical proportions. What matters, however, is that these strata are predisposed to perceive this peril as serious, pressing, and protean. Counterrevolutionaries play on this predisposition by misrepresenting every strike or demonstration as evidence of a controlled and sinister revolutionary design. Particularly in the wake of prolonged disorders or abortive insurrections, they prevail on traumatized conservatives and reactionaries to acquiesce, if not join, in a pre-emptive assault on exhausted and dispirited revolutionaries. Counterrevolutionaries claim that this preventive blow is necessary in order to make sure that momentarily disabled revolutionaries should not regroup their forces for another challenge to law and order.

At no stage do the leaders of an ascendant counterrevolutionary movement envisage or mount a frontal challenge to the existing regime and authority system. Rather, no matter how extensive their popular base, they seek and bid for the cooperation of strategic leaders and segments of the incumbent society, economy, and government. It is this strategy, which also dictates the equivocations of their socioeconomic program, that so clearly distinguishes the counterrevolutionary from the revolutionary project.

The masters of counterrevolution have no illusions about the vulnerability of state and government to direct frontal attack. It is almost as if they, rather than the socialists, assimilated the warnings of Engels about the impossibility of toppling modern regimes in peacetime.

By 1895, Engels was certain that in the future insurgents would be at a growing disadvantage when battling loyal government units in the streets and at the barricades. All the technical, organizational, and tactical innovations increasingly favored regular military and police forces, while "all the conditions on the insurgents' side have grown worse." Engels concluded that the "time of surprise attacks, of revolutions carried through by small conscious minorities at the head of unconscious masses," was past.

This being so, he cautioned socialists against playing with insurrection, against letting themselves be driven into premature street fighting, in which the forces of order would have all the advantages. Only a new world crisis could again open the road to revolutions from below, and until then, the period of revolutions from above would continue.

With or without the benefit of such insights from the opposing side, counterrevolutionaries are nothing if they are not advocates and students of the exercise of violence in politics. They realize that even their drilled paramilitary units and regimented mass movement will not allow them to measure themselves against efficient and loyal military and police units. They know that the authorities will go to almost any length to maintain their monopoly on the use of violence, which defines their legitimate sovereignty.

These authorities—central, regional, local—have it in their power to prevent, contain, and repress those who challenge them. Whatever their changing strategy or tactic of control, they have the technical and organizational resources to make any degree of intended force effective. The limits on this use of force, far from being material, are political, legal, and ethical.

Counterrevolutionary leaders are fully aware of these restraints on any government's recourse to coercion. Accordingly, they resolve to persuade individuals and groups to press for a discretion favorable to themselves. By exhortation, cajolery, and intimidation they prevail on them to favor the counterrevolutionary cause within governmental, judicial, and ecclesiastic institutions.

In normal times, the personnel of these institutions is relatively undivided; it also claims that its functions, which are directed to the maintenance of order and system, are politically neutral, are "above" politics. Crisis conditions undermine this harmony and dispute this pretense. At all levels, but most consequentially at the higher echelons, government functionaries, both civil and military, court officers, and church dignitaries become politicized: they are reminded of their social station as well as of their class and family ties, and they begin to make partisan choices. *i.e., they become "conscious"*

This political activation results in the emergence of significant individuals and factions within these institutions that, even without prompting by counterrevolutionaries, sympathize with their cause and are prepared to use their official influence and power in its behalf. These actors and groups may or may not declare themselves formally and publicly. What matters is that they impel their respective institutions to exercise discrimination in favor of the counterrevolutionary project.

Of course, the intensity and effectiveness of these procounterrevolutionary impulses are affected by a variety of factors. Depending on the method and pattern of recruitment, the critical cadres of bureaucracy, army, court, and church have greater or lesser affinities and ties—family, social, economic—with the upper cartel of anxiety and stagnation and with the middle crisis strata. But even in countries in which these interconnections are important, their political potency is heavily conditioned by the operative political ethos, culture, and system. This larger political context will determine the degree to which civil and military officials can and do exercise their influence and power to effect and implement policies advantageous to counterrevolutionaries.

Times of crisis foment politically charged tensions and divisions within vital segments of the executive branch of government. And, more important, soaring party and factional conflicts make for cabinet instability at the same time that they weaken the legislative controls of the executive. Inevitably, this cabinet instability and legislative paralysis redound to the benefit of high-ranking permanent officials in those ministries that have the primary responsibility for the enforcement of law and order.

It is precisely among these officials of the ministries of the interior, justice, and war, as well as in key commands of the police and army, that counterrevolutionary sympathies are most likely to manifest themselves. Officials and officers of such sympathies tend to have political connections outside their services. These are designed to strengthen their position within their respective institutions as well as, if need be, against intractable cabinet superiors. Again, the structure of the authority system decides whether these politicized civil servants seek or receive support from court circles, upper chambers, conservative and reactionary parties or factions, interest or pressure groups, and the ecclesiastic hierarchy.

When a crisis situation assumes grave proportions, especially in the minds of the power and ruling elites, an incumbent government of pragmatic and liberal conservatives is besieged on three sides: real or alleged revolutionaries who threaten disorder or insurrection; counterrevolutionaries who from the streets and the piazzas apply pressure for tough measures; and high civil servants and officers who set overbearing conditions for their continuing loyalty.

If its own popular and legislative power is also being eroded just then, this cross fire leaves the government little choice. Lack of regular, tested support undermines its ability to force the implementation of an even-handed internal security policy toward revolutionaries as well as counterrevolutionaries. Afraid of being left without any effective shield against the alleged revolution, the incumbent cabinet buys the continuing services of internal security agencies at the price of allowing them to carry out policies of differential surveillance, containment, and repression. Under these circumstances, even pragmatic and liberal conservatives wind up condoning a policy of stern control of revolutionaries and one of barely hidden license for counterrevolutionaries.

In countries with thoroughly authoritarian political systems, not only is there at best a marginal chance of revolutionary forces posing any real threat, but also the repressive machinery works so effectively that there is limited need or scope for outright counterrevolutionary action. Similarly, in a parliamentary country in which the social and political foundations of pragmatic conservatism remain solid and unbending even in the face of a real or presumed revolutionary threat, counterrevolutionary forays are contained and their inroads remain latent and disguised. In both instances, however, counterrevolutionary ingredients become a part of the offensively vigilant posture of conservatives and reactionaries, particularly if there are counterrevolutionary advances in neighboring countries.

In sum, counterrevolutionary leaders know that if they are to build their movement and seize power they have to blunt or neutralize the state's means of coercion against them. Accordingly, at the same time that they seek to influence conservatives and reactionaries in their favor in the wider political and social arena, they also seek tolerance and cooperation in the civil and military bureaucracy. Since crisis conditions activate and reinforce the built-in conservative and reactionary biases of law-enforcement and order-keeping agencies, they find it relatively easy to enlist auxiliaries there.

Counterrevolutionaries hope that these respondents will exert themselves on their behalf within their services as well as within government circles. Specifically, they want them to make sure that their semi-legal and illegal politics of the street, including their terror, is dealt with leniently. They rely on these auxiliaries to see to it that their organizations are not outlawed; that their rallies and demonstrations are not banned; that their punitive raids are not forestalled or broken up prematurely; and that their toughs are not sternly prosecuted, convicted, and sentenced. Counterrevolutionaries do not need outright patronage and aid. What they hope for and get is benevolent neutrality, calculated inaction, and furtive partiality.

Before the seizure of power, this combination of passivity, indifference, and protection near the center of government is perhaps best revealed in the relative immunity of counterrevolutionary terrorism. As compared to the red terror, the white terror tends to be better organized and more systematic; to strike at persons rather than things; to be executed by vicious rather than self-sacrificing fanatics; and to be integral rather than peripheral to the over-all project.

Even so, the terrorist units and circles of counterrevolutionary movements are not likely to be infiltrated by undercover agents, paid informers, and *agents provocateurs;* or, in the event that they are, this penetration remains relatively innocuous. Because of different degrees of police connivance, perpetrators and accomplices of individual acts of white terror have a better chance of eluding arrest than their red counterparts. And if arrested, there is every chance that they will be brought before indulgent magistrates, prosecutors, and judges. Even though these officials endorse neither their ultimate purposes nor their crude methods, many of them do have pronounced antipathies for the targets and victims of the white terror. The defense plays on these with consummate skill, encasing its pleas for clemency in ideas and language drawn from the conservative decalogue. The result is that the penalties, even for proven assassins, tend to be rather short prison sentences. If these are not instantly reprieved or suspended, the prisoners can still look forward to an early pardon or release. Should any of them seek their freedom through escape, their jail breaks are rarely of the sort that result in prisoners "being shot while trying to escape."

In the wake of pogroms, punitive raids, and street battles, the initiators and perpetrators of such collective violence tend to be punished much less severely than those of their victims who have the temerity to defend themselves. Soldiers or policemen, possibly after first holding the ring, may well finally intervene to put an end to such illegal disturbances. If they do, whatever

excesses they commit while restoring order are more likely to
fall upon the resisters than the assailants. In addition, the
authorities, both political and judicial, are particularly prone to
wink at such uneven and prejudiced police brutality, which is
so easily justified as the unfortunate yet inevitable and random
cost of law enforcement.

For reasons discussed above, incumbent governments may not
be able or willing to correct this tendentious law enforcement
and political justice. While the state thus tacitly invests the counterrevolutionary project with a political sanction, religious leaders consecrate it spiritually by their own accommodating
behavior.

The church is one of the principal pillars, if not the linchpin,
not only of conservatism, but also of reaction. Though by no
means monolithic, its over-all thrust is in support of conservative
and reactionary forces and ideas, as well as of existing social and
political institutions. Although prominent churchmen may oppose
incumbent governments, they almost never systematically question the regime as such. Wherever the throne survives, the
principal altar is at the royal palace. But in other types of
regimes, the clergy also ceremonially sanctifies the flag, the
army, and the chief executive. By both doctrine and temperament it preaches dutiful quiescence to the silent masses and
watchful collaboration to the attentive publics. Many leading
church dignitaries have close associations with the ruling class,
and they share its ways of thinking as well as its formulas for
secular action.

In times of crisis, the ecclesiastical leaders have all the same
intensely preservative reflexes as the conservative and reactionary
elites, from whom they do not dare separate. All feed on and
respond alike to the fear of revolution. Provided counterrevolutionary leaders are resolutely antirevolutionary, church leaders
bear with the latter's erratic anticlericalism, which is part of the
drive to discredit traditional institutions and authority patterns,
including the religious ones. This ecclesiastic abnegation further
undercuts the resilience of conservatives: once their ultra-nation-
alist thunder is stolen by counterrevolutionaries, they are left
only with religious appeals with which to rally popular support.

With these appeals compromised by the political behavior of their chief custodians, the ideological effectiveness of conservatism in strife-torn societies is jeopardized still further.

At any rate, no matter how areligious or antireligious, counterrevolutionaries are careful not to break outright with the major established churches. Similarly, no matter how irritated, offended, and worried by the paganism, blasphemy, and incivility of the counterrevolutionaries, churchmen refrain from denouncing or excommunicating them. At critical moments the churches actually provide the spiritual benison for the united front of conservatism, reaction, and counterrevolution.

As for the universities, they too are an integral part of the conservational complex. Whether governmental or private, their overseers and administrators, as well as their professors, have multiple relations, interests, values, perceptions, and functions that tie them to the ruling and possessing classes. Because of the prevailing patterns of access and recruitment to higher education, the same holds true for the vast majority of students. To be sure, the situation is never totally undiversified and undeviating. In the churches segments of the lower clergy and the flock may now and then register philorevolutionary sympathies and pressures, whereas in the universities segments of the junior faculty and student body may occasionally turn philorevolutionary in both thought and action.

In that event, however, the responses of regnant university cadres will tend to be aligned with those of the conservative establishment at large. To forestall any doubts about their own loyalties, professors issue timely disclaimers of affinity with rebels. But before too long they may also denounce, if not inform against real or presumed *enragés*, while at the same time warning that militancy can only play into the hands of forces calling for the unrestrained and pre-emptive repression of dissent, within the university and beyond.

When dealing with militant counterrevolutionaries and their sympathizers, this same professoriate, together with other attached or dependent intellectuals and experts, is less inclined to force the pace of disavowal, reprobation, and foreboding. It tends to take cues from and emulate the conduct of nonacademic conservatives. If these gloss over the threatened and actual excesses of counterrevolutionaries at the same time that they fulminate against revolutionaries, more than likely university establishments will follow suit. The result of this one-sided censure of immoderation is to involve the prestige of yet another morally and ethically freighted institution in the differential evaluation and reprobation of revolutionary and counterrevolutionary extremism, including violence. Again, the counterrevolutionary cause benefits from a purposive silence that is pregnant with tacit approval.

All in all, counterrevolutionary leaders, ideas, and movements, unlike their revolutionary counterparts, are firmly anchored in incumbent government, society, and economy, as well as being deeply imbedded in the overlapping matrices of conservatism and reaction. In style, method, and appearance their break with the politics of compromise and mutual concession is very radical indeed. But in all other major respects the counterrevolutionary project is in the nature of a stabilizing and rescue operation disguised as a millenarian crusade of heroic vitalism.

The major vested interests, conservative and reactionary political formations, and the government's internal security agencies could hardly be expected to oppose this protective thrust. Not that they ever support it outright or consistently. National conditions and conjunctural developments define their changing relationships with the ascendant counterrevolution. Moreover, although these interests, formations, and agencies are interconnected and interdependent, they never cease to quarrel and compete among themselves. As a result, their shifts in policies and alignments are not readily synchronized. Counterrevolutionary leaders capitalize on this intra-elite conflict as much as feuding conservatives and reactionaries threaten each other with instant overtures to counterrevolutionaries. The convergent interest groups, governmental camarillas, and political parties that engage in this intramural rivalry have one structural characteristic in common: in all of them a small core of leaders can make decisions for their respective constituencies without any great risk of being disavowed. Consequently even relatively minor mutations in the policy and influence of a few key actors can result in rather large and momentous changes in the over-all political constellation and climate.

This jockeying for position within the antirevolutionary triad becomes particularly intense and critical when counterrevolutionaries seek to press their advantage in moments of acute crisis, either real or imagined, unpremeditated or contrived. With the center in eclipse, the greater the revolutionary pressures and influences, both immediate and anticipated, the greater the bargaining power of the counterrevolutionary leaders, whose instruments of control are coveted by unsettled conservatives and reactionaries in and out of government. In other words, the fate of the counterrevolutionary movement in no small measure depends on the resilience of its collaborating yet rival conservative and reactionary partners.

Ultimately, then, the power and governing elites play a pivotal role in the Janus-faced crisis that harbors revolution as well as counterrevolution. It is their interests and needs as well as their power, influence, self-confidence, and decisions that frame the parameters in which such crises are resolved.

Certainly in terms of their socioeconomic bases, political allies, and governmental abettors, counterrevolutionaries are tied into the conservative-reactive constellation. As for their program of economic and social reform, "its studied prevarication "stems from these same preservative and retrogressive taproots. Counterrevolutionary leaders strike for a fundamental political overturn that is neither contingent upon nor prelude to any consequential changes in economic, social, and class relations, values, and institutions. In actual fact, more likely than not these economic and social arrangements are shored up. It is as if the besieged establishment earns this reinforcement in consideration for past political favors and concessions. Except in the political sphere, whatever ground is reinforced or reclaimed reverts to conservatives and reactionaries, and not to their counterrevolutionary partners.

The counterrevolution's fitful but indispensable association with weighty personalities and institutions of the establishment —both governmental and nongovernmental—attests to its intrinsically conservative orientation as well as to the striking

duality of its methods. In their drive for influence and power
counterrevolutionary leaders use changeable blends of legitimate
and illegitimate political methods, of old and new political styles,
of archaic and modern political rhetoric. This contrived mixture
is further evidence of the interstitial emplacement of the counterrevolutionary project: for political support it looks both upward
and downward; for ideological inspiration backward and forward; and for historical ratification to itself and its would-be
partners.

Because of its composite, interjacent, and contingent qualities
the counterrevolutionary project lacks ecumenical luster or mag-
netism. Unlike its revolutionary counterpart, whose liberating
and transcending principles have a universal resonance, it com-
mends itself by the example of its praxis.

As they feel their way counterrevolutionary leaders of different countries at first pay only casual attention to one another's
pragmatic search for effective political formulas. Although oper-
ating in widely disparate national contexts, they experiment with
homologous programmatic appeals and organizational weapons.
Beginning in the 1870s, all over Europe inflamed and truculent
nationalism emerges as the sole, self-flattering affirmation in ideological platforms that otherwise bristle with negations. These
platforms also accuse the ruling and tone-setting establishment
of pandering to advancing and corroding modernism, of fostering
divisive factionalism, and of tolerating subversive conspiracies
at home. In turn, these internal cankers are said to be both cause
and effect of debasing pusillanimity in foreign, including imperial, affairs.

Premature counterrevolutionaries grope and probe for methods
to generate and frame mass support for those political actors and
institutions that seem peculiarly prone and suited to spearhead
firm resistance to the forces of reform and revolution. With new-
fledged appeals of nationalism, anti-Semitism, racism, economic
meliorism, and social imperialism, they seek to rally traditionally
silent or apathetic strata around the king or would-be king, the
"reliable" legislative or ministerial council (notably the upper
house), the army, the bureaucracy, and the church. Since counterrevolutionary leaders denounce parties and party politics for

undermining the unity of state and society, they undertake to organize their new recruits in leagues and movements; and they claim that these stand above party and class. In other words, they neither ignore nor reject those innovations in political mobilization and organization that are designed for times of growing popular participation. Rather, they propose to exploit and adjust the new methods of mass politics for their own purposes.

At first these purposes do not include the construction of an independent power base from which to launch an assault for exclusive control of state and government. Instead, the minimum objective is to restore the backbone of conservatives and reactionaries in and out of government who, only against their own better judgments and interests, have been acquiescing in the pragmatic conservatism of gradual but continual and linear change. These are the political, social, and economic actors whom counterrevolutionaries seek to prod into resistance. They are told that there are political strategies and tactics that do not require endless concessions which, over time, fatally erode prestigious but superannuated classes, status groups, interests, and institutions.

Needless to say, some pessimistic notables counsel policies of outright repression. As part of a coup from the right, such traditional hard-liners urge the arrest and proscription of revolutionaries and their sympathizers; the restriction of the franchise; the curb of legislative controls of the executive; or the revitalization of the beleaguered yet compliant upper chamber.

Though these time-honored stratagems are never totally precluded, they are viewed skeptically for not being adapted to conditions of mass politics. Counterrevolutionaries are peculiarly sensitive to the popular requirements and potentials of resistance to history. They come forth to establish highly charged political links between, on the one hand, insulated, overextended, and arrogant elites, and, on the other hand, impassive, insecure, and resentful middle urban and rural strata. Whereas the former distrust and recoil from popular politics, the latter are indifferent to it. Counterrevolutionaries, for their part, face it confidently and boldly.

Depending on the authority and constitutional system, counterrevolutionaries not only hail the limited franchise but may actually press for the adoption of universal suffrage. They trust themselves, their slogans, and their campaign methods to summon up large segments of the enfranchised crisis strata in support of the antirevolutionary cause. They mean to bring them to the polls to vote for either outright counterrevolutionary candidates or for compatible conservative or reactionary office-seekers.

According to Robert Michels, "a party of the landed gentry which would appeal only to the members of its own class and to those of identical economic interests, would not win a single seat, would not send a single representative to parliament." Half-mockingly, Michels adds that "a conservative candidate who should present himself to his electors by declaring to them that he did not regard them as capable of playing an active part in influencing the destinies of the country, and should tell them that for this reason they ought to be deprived of the suffrage, would be a man of incomparable sincerity, but politically insane."

Clearly, the old ruling groups have no alternative but to "descend, during the elections, from their lofty seats, and to avail themselves of the same democratic and demagogic methods" as those employed by the organized proletariat. "The conservative spirit of the old mastercaste, however deeply rooted it may be, is forced to assume, at least during times of election, a specious democratic mask."

It would seem that counterrevolutionaries, along with ideological conservatives and reactionaries—rather than poised conservatives and reactionaries—are the ones to "descend" into the electoral arena and to don that "specious democratic mask." It is they, furthermore, who launch, forge, and manage the new leagues and movements. Again, depending on the national context, these can be vote-getting machines, pressure groups, ideological generators, direct-action units, or any combination thereof. But whatever the blend of their functions and the social composition of their membership, these novel political formations are offshoots as well as licensed or unwitting auxiliaries of the conservative-reactive constellation of power.

More likely than not, some of the principal initiators of such formations are sometime renegades from natural conservatism or reaction. Prominent conservatives and reactionaries sit on the executive committee, provide funds, and generally lend their prestige. Not that intramural relations are at all times harmonious and mutually supportive. Especially in the early phases, when leagues or movements are inchoate, pragmatic conservative and reactionary political actors and parties are in a position to dictate the terms of collaboration. In the light of changing political requirements, they enlist, decline, or spurn the support of such fledgling organizations; or advertise, conceal, or deny the affinities and affiliations that tie them to their auxiliaries.

This relationship remains one-sided until leagues or movements acquire countervailing leverage and prove their own political muscle and mettle. Their bargaining position improves with their growing membership; with their success in effecting the general climate of opinion through rallies, newspapers, pamphlets, petitions, and punitive raids; and with their ability to muster sympathizers and fellow travelers among influentials throughout the establishment, including the government.

In addition, certain political conjunctures benefit the counterrevolutionaries, particularly in times of deepening crisis. Eventually reformists and liberal conservatives press the government and right-wing parties to openly repudiate the objectives, methods, and leaders of these leagues and movements. But office-holders hesitate to do so, fearful that this attack on their auxiliaries is part of a larger offensive against themselves. The net result is that counterrevolutionaries become impressed with their own indispensability and set progressively steeper conditions for their future cooperation with the upper cartel of anxiety. The result is the same when, in moments of panic, a conservative government and its supporting parties and factions spur the leagues and movements to redouble their activities.

In other words, during the embryonic phase, precocious counterrevolutionaries are likely to be on the lookout for helpful and adaptable ideological, programmatic, and strategic innovations in other countries. Overall, however, they improvise and test their projects in rigorously national, regional, and local settings, without ever contemplating a break with the conservative-reactive complex, whose parentage they could not deny.

But this national encapsulation and filial obeisance wear thin when chronic tensions and disorders are aggravated by recurrent jolts whose scope and mainsprings transcend national borders. Indeed, each national crisis becomes a ward of a much larger international crisis, and turns into a local expression as well as a stimulant of the symbiotically structured encounter of revolution and counterrevolution that refuses to respect geographic frontiers. Once a revolution or counterrevolution has scored a breakthrough in any one country, the dramatis personae on all sides realize that hereafter they will be performing in political theaters with stages that have been internationalized. The mere existence of a model is enough to stimulate political actors to locate themselves in relation to it by positive, qualified, or negative imitation. Moverover, the existence of an international vanguard base opens up the possibility of various forms of external aid for struggling revolutionary or counterrevolutionary movements. From another perspective, this prospect and solicitation for assistance from across the borders looks like foreign intervention.

But whether aid or intervention, this external entanglement is central to the international civil war of an historical era that is as counterrevolutionary as it is revolutionary. When vanguard bases provide aid or intervene, they do so in response to varying degrees of prior solicitation, and with varying degrees of intentionality and directness. A vast range of factors determines not only the scale but also the nature (financial, political, technical, military) of this assistance to or interference in third countries.

But there is another question: what are the chances for survival of a first-born revolution or counterrevolution, particularly if it occurs in a small country? No vanguard regime, certainly no pioneering revolutionary regime, can count on the support or protection of sympathetic foreign governments. In fact, because of its potentially unsettling impact beyond its borders, such a regime instantly prepares for adverse reactions from other governments. At a minimum, it seeks to exploit and foster those diplomatic rivalries and political complications which promise to either delay or minimize hostile foreign intervention.

The situation is altogether different when a revolution or counterrevolution unfolds in a small land *after* rather than before a kindred breakthrough in another, notably in a relatively close-by major country. Naturally a first-born revolution or counterrevolution that is carried by a big or medium power is less vulnerable to external diplomatic, economic, and military pressures. Moreover, the revolutionary or counterrevolutionary movement or regime of a major power has the incentive and capability to extend covert or open aid to second-born kindred movements or regimes in smaller countries. In turn, such a big-power umbrella animates revolutionary or counterrevolutionary movements and regimes in small countries to involve themselves in the internal struggles of their neighbors.

Obviously, the fortunes of second-born revolutionary or counterrevolutionary movements or regimes are significantly governed by the total international environment of their day. Indeed, one of the chief earmarks of any second-born revolution or counterrevolution is that, unlike its first-born predecessor, it is inspired and helped from outside. The issue is not whether it wants, requests, or receives aid. It is rather a question of the degree to which it does, and, if there is more than one external source, from which source. There are, of course, second-born revolutions or counterrevolutions whose ascendancy or survival is for the most part contingent upon external intervention. When this is the case, the aid or intervention of the sponsoring foreign power is fully apparent.

4. Varieties of Counterrevolution

Because of the great diversity of local conditions in which it erupts, the counterrevolutionary phenomenon has many faces. It may be useful, therefore, to differentiate seven varieties of counterrevolution: (1) pre-emptive, (2) posterior, (3) accessory, (4) disguised, (5) anticipatory, (6) externally licensed, and (7) externally imposed.

A _pre-emptive counterrevolution_ is most likely to make headway in polities and societies that have either just experienced an abortive revolution or a flood of far-reaching reforms, or else are in the midst of protracted governmental instability, fraught with explosive dangers. In an atmosphere heavy with suspicion, uncertainty, and abeyant violence, counterrevolutionary leaders try to convince embattled and traumatized elites that it is merely a matter of time until revolutionaries will again exploit the situation for their purposes. But rather than apply themselves to cooling the overheated atmosphere, they do their best to inflame it further. They do so in order to buttress their claim that revolution is imminent, while at the same time looking for, if not precipitating, confrontations in which to demonstrate their capacity to put down real or alleged revolutionaries. Conjuring up the dangers of leaving revolutionaries the time to prepare their forces and plans for an assault on _their_ terms, counterrevolutionary leaders urge a preventive thrust. Their rationale is that at worst such a strike would goad and force revolutionaries and their cohorts into battle before they were ready; at best it would catch them sufficiently off balance so that they would neither choose nor dare to offer serious resistance. In either event, the initiative would be squarely with the forces of law and order, thanks to the advantage of both surprise and preparation.

As noted above, counterrevolutionary leaders intentionally exaggerate the magnitude and imminence of the revolutionary threat. Moreover, and this was noted before as well, influential conservatives and reactionaries incline to accept this exaggeration for their own motives and purposes. Whether out of genuine fear, rational examination, purposeful political and class calculation, or, what is most likely, a combination of all of these, they endorse the call for a pre-emptive strategy. Whereas tormented center-leftists reprove revolutionaries and *enragés* for playing into the hands of counterrevolutionaries with their militancy and their refusal to close ranks, progressively fewer conservatives preach restraint to their potential auxiliaries.

These conservatives are besieged on all sides: by an ominous revolutionary challenge; by dwindling support for the politics of compromise and accommodation; and by mounting counterrevolutionary pressures from the streets as well as from within the government and bureaucracy. In addition, the urgency of the situation and the gravity of the policy alternatives intensify divisions within leading conservative and government circles. There is now sharp disagreement about how to handle the immediate impasse, more particularly about the wisdom and expediency of embarking on a pre-emptive course. At the same time, major factions of the old elites suspect each other of making separate deals with the counterrevolutionaries in pursuit of partisan advantage. In other words, they do not easily pull together and rally forces to block and bridle the counterrevolutionaries and their fellow travelers. Instead, preoccupied with their sway within the larger cartel of anxiety, conservatives and reactionaries slither onto a course that falls halfway between sparing and courting the counterrevolutionaries. Incidentally, few, if any, of their weighty notables ever seriously consider a rapprochement with moderate reformists with a view to shoring up the sagging vital center.

At any rate, counterrevolutionaries ingeniously play on these intra-elite and intra-governmental rivalries. At the same time they escalate their defiant pressures. Worried about the consequences of further disaggregation and disorder, competing factions of the upper cartel of anxiety resign themselves to composing their intramural differences for the purpose of making joint overtures to the counterrevolutionaries. Of course, they expect the counterrevolutionaries to settle for a subordinate role in the antirevolutionary directorate. They are stunned when these auxiliaries, who developed by their suffrance, hold out for first place.

It would be well to reiterate here that conservatives and reactionaries in and out of government are disinclined to enter into formal collaboration with counterrevolutionaries. Moreover, when they finally and grudgingly yield the supreme command posts to them, they do so for what they mean to be a limited purpose and time. In fact, they assume that they can raise counterrevolutionaries into the political saddle without ever surrendering to them the real and ultimate reins of power. While in the saddle the counterrevolutionaries are expected to restore and revitalize law and order for the foreseeable future. To achieve this objective, they are licensed to use whatever methods they deem necessary. But the moment this mission is accomplished, counterrevolutionaries are expected to dismount from the saddle voluntarily; to fall from it by their own incompetence; or to be forced out of it by conservatives and reactionaries who retain sufficient power, influence, and prestige to win any such test of strength.

This summons to the counterrevolutionary leaders to head up the government is in the nature of a quasi legal coup d'état from above. In a formal sense, the procedure does not violate the letter of the existing constitution. The collaboration and sanction of the highest civil and military authorities attest to this legality. While throwing open the front doors to power, this collaboration simultaneously disguises the degree to which counterrevolutionary leaders applied pressure from the streets and the piazzas to pry themselves into power.

But whatever the legal and political maneuvers surrounding this transfer of authority, these merely provide the context and platform, not the scope, for the exercise of that authority. At first it might seem as if the counterrevolutionaries would proceed or be licensed to invest their rule with only as much power as they and their patrons consider necessary to restore and secure order. It quickly becomes apparent, however, that the political dynamic of this operation is of an entirely different nature. It is not the requirements of repression but the ratios and conflicts of power within the antirevolutionary camp that determine whether or not the coup from above develops into an outright counterrevolutionary regime.

Insofar as the revolutionary danger is *real*, it can easily be crushed by the application of commensurate force and violence, particularly if the army and police remain loyal. But counterrevolutionaries and their conservative and reactionary associates are not concerned with *actual* hazards. They are haunted by a ubiquitous and hydra-headed specter that eludes destruction or decapitation. To the extent that they manage to manipulate the specter, they can call for ever more stringent internal security measures and for iron vigilance.

The counterrevolutionaries realize that their partners and patrons share their deliberate misrepresentation and defamation of reformers and advanced liberals as revolutionaries or insidious fellow travelers. They also know that their co-partners are eager for them to cleanse the country of all revolutionaries and their organizations and to restrict all rights and channels of political expression and interest aggregation. As a pledge of their own economic and social conservatism, the counterrevolutionary leaders curb the champions of social reform in their own ranks. Equivocal as it was, their reformist rhetoric did help to mobilize mass support. But at this new juncture the populist *enragés* of the counterrevolutionary movement threaten to do more harm than good by feeding the establishment's residual suspicions of the socioeconomic purposes of its presumed helpmates.

Having been accorded the sought-after free hand in the political sphere, the counterrevolutionaries must prove their competence not only in the suppression of revolutionaries but also in the running of the state apparatus. In other words, they cannot pursue the extension of their power base at the expense of performing essential government functions and services. This is particularly true because they assume power at a time of paralyzing breakdowns—economic, fiscal, social, and political—that require government action if they are to be repaired.

It is in this vital aspect of their rule that the counterrevolutionaries benefit from the stanch and interested collaboration of the old cadres, including or especially of their topmost echelons.

Notwithstanding the friction inherent to this cooperation, by dutifully staying in their posts and manning them efficiently, these cadres provide the experts and the expertise that are in such short supply in the counterrevolutionary ranks.

Admittedly, here and there prominent officials are cashiered or reassigned to less sensitive posts because their loyalty is suspect. What matters, however, is that nearly all high civil servants, military and police officers, judges, teachers, foreign-office officials, and diplomats sympathize in various degrees with the principal purposes that their new political superiors claim to champion. For that reason they are not only willing but eager to facilitate the changing of the political guard, to serve as a guarantee of continuity, and to devise and implement policies designed, as a first step, to restabilize their country's domestic and foreign situation. Indeed, without their duteous collaboration —for whatever motive or reason—the legitimacy and governmental tenure of the counterrevolutionaries would be seriously jeopardized. Both depend on quick results, some flashier than real, in the realms of employment, income, "law" enforcement, and diplomacy. Key private sectors, which all along advocated, or at least never obstructed, the transfer of power, also cooperate in the restoration of conditions favorable to themselves.

Simultaneously, the new government leaders and their party associates prepare and gradually implement the conversion of an essentially authoritarian coup and government into a counterrevolutionary regime that is both caesaristic and doctrinaire. They can now combine the leverage stemming from their governmental positions with the political influence, power, and coercion rooted in their movement and paramilitary units. They use these two levers to consolidate their monopoly in the political sphere. The counterrevolutionary leaders seek exclusive control of the government machinery, of all checks on the government, and of mass communications. To achieve and secure this ambitious goal, they spin such a complicated web of controls and sanctions that the political movement and the government lose their separate sovereignties and, except in terms of status and career opportunities, become thoroughly entwined. The old ruling groups continue to find status and promotion in the bureaucracy and regular armed services, while the client crisis strata seek and find social and economic opportunity primarily in the parallel yet interlocked party organizations, both civil and military.

Significantly, this fundamental restructuring of politics, government, and communications proceeds without any consequential changes in class structure and property relations. Nor are the status, mobility, and deference patterns basically altered. In fact, as a trade-off for monopolistic control in the political realm and for parallel preserves for social and economic advancement, the established classes and status groups are left undisturbed. Big industry, big agriculture, and the churches are kept in line by a combination of bribery and intimidation. All three are grateful for the restoration of stability, the suppression of revolutionaries, and the emasculation of organized labor. Provided their leaders and spokesmen agree to abstain from or be compliant in politics, they are promised not only immunity but even government support. Intimidation takes the form of threatening the denial of autonomy, preferment, and profits.

There is, then, a transformation in politics and government coincident with a consolidation of economy, society, and church. Within the governmental sphere, parallel structures with overlapping jurisdictions tend to be personified in key officials whose first allegiance is to the leaders of the ruling party. Likewise, the links between this governmental sphere and the autonomous socioeconomic orbit are managed by party officials who are superordinate, not impartial, brokers.

The incongruities of this superstructural transformation and infrastructural permanence are hidden by a mounting nationalist frenzy grafted on to a soaring fear of the specter of revolution and subversion. At the same time, these incongruities are reduced by a gradual militarization that bolsters the economy while embodying the nationalist revival. Specifically, rearmament provides contracts, profits, and jobs within the existing economic framework. It enables the old ruling and strategic elites and the new political elites to promote and benefit from economic recovery without divisive partisan battles over income redistribution and tax reform.

Of course, at first rearmament is only one of a number of pump-priming methods and is considerably less salient than the uniforms, flags, and parades that characterize the general militarization. But once the economy again begins to deteriorate, war production ceases to be a mere lubricant of the economy and of political stability: it becomes a principal mainstay. The ascendant military-industrial complex develops overlapping as well as competing public and private sectors, with party officials manning the switches at critical points of intersection and conflict.

Needless to say, the more years that elapse without any concerted challenge to the encroaching monopoly of political power and control, the more difficult such a challenge becomes. Not only are revolutionary, reformist, and liberal political organizations destroyed or crippled but, equally important, the political formations of conservatism and reaction tend to atrophy from lack of activity, influence, and patronage. At the same time that they crush their opponents politically and politically castrate their coadjutors, the counterrevolutionary leaders harden their own political machinery and popular support.

By the time restabilization begins to falter, the coadjutors find themselves locked in. To be sure, they become increasingly appalled by their own political subordination, if not servility, and by the repressive methods, including terror, of the new men of power. But they are unnerved not only because their own political formations are devitalized but also because they have surrendered whatever mass appeals and following they may have had. Uncertain, as always, of their own ability to marshal popular support in moments of crisis, conservatives and reactionaries continue to condone the excesses of the mass movement from the right rather than take any chances, however remote, on the revival of any mass movement from the left.

In any case, the old ruling classes and strategic elites are confined to their economic, professional, social, ecclesiastic, and bureaucratic enclaves. All along they share the incumbent government's proclivity to narrow and bridge over festering and potentially unsettling breakdowns, disaffections, and cleavages by stepping up diplomatic scrimmages and rearmament.

Although they may eventually develop second thoughts about their contribution to the juggernaut that is heading for diversionary war, the class and status interests and the self-inflicted political impotence of these time-honored elites conspire to keep them complicit. Naturally enough, they tell themselves that they continue their collaboration so as to help prevent the worst by boring from within. In actual fact, this conservative and reactionary collaborationism has far deeper economic, social, and political roots than this rationalization suggests. And these roots are imbedded not only in national but also in international soil.

Compared with the pre-emptive counterrevolution, whose thrust is against an apparent but allegedly imminent revolution or revolutionary peril, the *posterior counterrevolution* is directed against a real but external revolutionary target. It develops in response to a successful yet still contested revolution.

The target to be attacked is of one of three kinds: the revolutionary regime of an insurgent city; a revolutionary regime that controls the capital and large sections of a country but is caught up in civil war; or a revolutionary regime that is in control of an entire country.

In all three instances, military force is the cutting edge of the campaign aimed at overthrowing and crushing a fragile revolutionary regime. When investing an insurgent city, a "legitimate" government raises regular troops, volunteers, and mercenaries in territories under its control. Foreign assistance tends to be limited, indirect, and nonmilitary.

Foreign aid or intervention is of altogether greater magnitude and importance in the other two types of posterior counterrevolutionary campaigns. In the case of civil war the white side secures money, equipment, supplies, and manpower from abroad, if possible along with diplomatic recognition. In the event of an assault against a country that is completely under the control of a revolutionary regime, the invading armies are almost entirely foreign.

The specifically counterrevolutionary impetus of each of these military campaigns depends on a wide range of factors. Most important, it is a function of the political make-up of the attacking government, the political and social orientation of the commanding generals, the social composition of their troops, and the nature and extent of the antirevolutinary forces that resurface to cooperate with the advancing ("liberating") armies.

Such head-on confrontations have a logic of their own. Whatever the political coloration of the opposing camps at the outset, with time the "ultras" on both sides tend to become ascendant, if not predominant.

The siege and hostile armies precipitate a *levée en masse* in the revolutionary fortress or behind the revolutionary lines. The attendant tightening of the revolutionary regime and discipline, punctuated by red terror, intensifies the suppression of undisguised antirevolutionaries and counterrevolutionaries. It also hastens the removal from government of militants who refuse to sacrifice revolutionary values and programs to the requirements of armed defense, and of fellow travelers who might serve as go-betweens in the search for a negotiated settlement.

A similar hardening process is at work on the opposing side. Even when the military campaign is under the direction of a centrist government, the elements favoring a frontal assault and unconditional surrender tend to impose themselves and their policies.

Because the military effort gets first priority, army generals acquire disproportionate influence not only in setting strategy but also in political affairs. Most if not all of these officers are fiercely antirevolutionary. They have close status and class ties with the leaders and organizations of the upper cartel of anxiety. Moreover, the volunteers and mercenaries serving under their command are drawn from or have close affinities with the intermediate crisis strata.

The old ruling elites—including generals, high civil servants, churchmen, and landed aristocrats—also achieve a paramount position in the émigré circles that form in the major capitals during a posterior counterrevolutionary campaign. They are the ones that have international connections, both political and social, which they now exploit on behalf of their cause. As the case may be, these émigrés solicit aid for their side in the civil war or lobby for foreign armies to be sent to "liberate" their country. Invariably they count on like-minded reactionaries and conservatives to pressure their governments to adopt policies favorable to them. Émigrés and whatever principals they may have back home prefer to solicit external aid from nations and governments that have no or at best marginal territorial designs on their country.

Evidently, neither the internal authorities organizing and directing a campaign to overthrow a revolutionary regime nor the foreign governments assisting them or mounting a drive of their own are of outright counterrevolutionary bent. Such enterprises are controlled by coalitions of activated conservatives and reactionaries. Whereas the former mean to restore the status quo ante, the latter propose to take advantage of this conjuncture to turn the historical clock back to an earlier time. Behind the screen of a tenuous political truce, these two factions jockey for position, their objective being to improve their chances for control of the "post-liberation" government. This intramural rivalry is affected by the course of military operations, the political developments in "liberated" territories, and, to a much lesser extent, the influence of supporting or commanding foreign governments.

But what about the importance and role of counterrevolutionaries as such? Needless to say, they do not figure prominently among the émigrés. Voluntary exile is a luxury that individuals of their modest social status and economic resources can ill afford. In addition, counterrevolutionary leaders lack the international contacts and cosmopolitan ways with which to gain access to the influentials of foreign capitals.

Besides, whereas conservatives and reactionaries come from and expect to return to established positions, counterrevolutionaries come forth in response to the requirements and opportunities of a fast-breaking situation. Civil and ideologically saturated war becomes fierce, brutal, and uncompromising on both sides. While in the revolutionary camp officers and especially soldiers rally around a liberating idea—which in case of foreign intervention is reinforced by nationalist appeals—the situation is rather different on the opposing side. There the civilian as well as the military leaders have a passionate sense of restorative or reactionary direction. But their efforts to translate their project into an ideology and program for instant mass mobilization miscarry. In fact, precisely because of the absence of ideas that can stir the multitudes to shoulder bayonets, the antirevolutionary crusade relies heavily on volunteers and mercenaries, most of whom are willful soldiers of fortune.

Military victory is a primary though essentially instrumental goal of all types of wars, whether civil or international. But the ultimate objectives of wars differ quite markedly. Traditional international conflicts are fought for territorial readjustments, material reparations, and possibly changes in the defeated enemy's government. Civil and ideologically charged wars revolve around questions of regime: revolutionaries seek to preserve their new regime while their enemies seek to destroy it completely and quickly.

While the besieged revolutionary regime is without solid institutional, social, and symbolic roots, the depth and intensity of the loyalty it arouses more than compensates for this lack of historical sanction. The soldiers of the antirevolution are asked not only to storm this fanatically held fortress but also to play an important role in the political warfare accompanying and following military operations. Certain units, officers, and men of the advancing armies consider themselves ordained to repress, punish, and wreak vengeance. The first phase of this white terror is capricious and uncontrolled, as are so many of the instant measures of political, economic, social, and religious restoration or reaction.

Both this white terror and this instant reclamation are distinguished by the reckless application of violence; and they are directed and executed by individuals who fit the social, economic, psychological, and political profile of counterrevolutionary actors.

This counterrevolutionary thrust is not easily reined in. Because the political directorate of an antirevolutionary campaign is so inchoate, it has difficulties controlling local commanders and units. In addition, the moment the prospects of victory improve or victory is won, intramural conflicts flare up, both at the center and locally. This infighting further impairs the effectiveness of political authorities. On the one hand, the directorate comes under mounting pressure from frenzied conservatives and reactionaries: they condone or even favor a policy of savage retribution to eradicate the last traces of rebellion and to set a deterrent example for the foreseeable future. In the field, on the other hand, the directorate is confronted with military and civilian personnel that is heartened by this "official" patronage for pitiless repression at the same time that it is reinforced by kindred elements that resurface or surface in the wake of "liberation."

Eventually, the "postliberation" government institutionalizes the white terror. The hastily formalized procedures for special military and civil tribunals give an appearance of fairness and legality, particularly in comparison with what went before. This regularization soothes the troubled conscience of the conservatives and reactionaries who run the government. It also reduces hostile reactions and representations from abroad.

Still, the fact remains that while eagerly reclaiming their public and private positions, the old ruling and strategic elites tolerate the white terror. To be sure, they themselves furnish few prosecutors, executioners, and jailers; they disclaim all responsibility for brutal excesses; and they seek to minimize the scope and vigor of the retribution. Even so, by not promptly reprimanding or dismissing perpetrators of Inquisition-like proceedings, the reestablished upper strata legitimize the white terror —from which they also benefit, however indirectly. Staid conservatives and reactionaries do not brave the break with their counterrevolutionary auxiliaries until they feel secure in their recovered power and influence in government, society, economy, and church.

Quite clearly, cooperation between the upper cartel of anxiety and the counterrevolutionaries is consequential though not identical in pre-emptive and posterior counteroperations. In the pre-emptive variety, because they dispose of regimented mass support and paramilitary units, counterrevolutionary leaders have the strength to dismiss their conservative and reactionary partners after these coadjutors have paved the way for them to sole control of the political authority system. In the posterior variety, conservatives and reactionaries keep the upper hand in considerable measure because instant counterrevolutionaries lack the tested leadership and mass organization to challenge them. After permitting these adventitious and raw counterrevolutionary levies to murder, execute, jail, deport, and ostracize real and presumed transgressors, the old ruling and strategic elites dismiss them. They can afford to do so once they have reestablished their control over the army and the internal security services, and also because they are confident that their discharged helpers will eagerly stand by for any future emergency.

The *accessory counterrevolution*, very much like the pre-emptive variety, is directed against a presumed revolution or against alleged revolutionaries; and very much like the posterior variety, it is temporarily licensed. Actually, it develops in the second phase of a countermovement that begins and ends as a military operation designed to restore and strengthen traditional elites and institutions.

Conservative and reactionary strata that have recently been swept from political power in a crisis-torn society fear that any further erosion of their positions will preclude their comeback, perhaps forever. Some of their spokesmen seize on every misstep of the insecure reformist government and forces that have assumed authority and charge them with preparing the ground and being the unwitting agents for the still threatening revolution. Anxiety about their own future prompts many conservatives and reactionaries to see government-initiated and government-sponsored programs for major social and econmic change as so many opening wedges for revolutionary transformations.

Select leaders of the displaced or endangered ruling caste resolve to deny the new administration the time to consolidate its control of the state apparatus and to implement its remedial policies. In particular, high military officers, who also have reason to fear for their positions and status, begin to prepare an early strike. They do so confident of the support, both actual and latent, of large segments of the landowning, industrial, and ecclesiastic strata.

The military masterminds of this frontal challenge plan an action whose surprise, efficiency, and swiftness is designed to unsettle the government, whose ability to command the loyalty and operations of military and police forces is untested. Accordingly, without ever worrying about mass support and without making contingent plans for prolonged fighting, a few generals, certain of their own garrisons, issue and set out to execute their pronunciamento.

It is only when the government unexpectedly parries the blow and the coup becomes the precipitant of civil war that the insurgent generals look around for supplementary battle instruments. Among these, two are of capital importance: the aid of foreign governments from abroad and the aid of counterrevolutionary forces from within.

The assistance from abroad is particularly critical immediately after the coup falters. Access to government funds, military arsenals, and vital stockpiles is either completely blocked or sharply restricted. Also, the areas under insurgent control may not be fertile ground for the recruitment, provisioning, and equipment of troops. Accordingly, foreign military, economic, and financial assistance enables the insurgent side to defend its enclaves while at the same time building the sinews of power for a sustained drive against government positions. Of course, this foreign aid, which includes not only military advisers and technicians, but also regular troops, is provided by counterrevolutionary regimes that have multiple reasons for bolstering the tottering rebellion. Among these is their leaders' eagerness to impress their followers and sympathizers at home and abroad with the transnationalism and dynamism of their movement. Besides, "la contrerévolution est un bloc." The defeat of any kindred movement, or of one that is perceived as such by ideological friends and foes alike, threatens to undermine the prestige of the counterrevolutionary project in all quarters.

Meanwhile, internally the insurgent leaders, both military and civilian, are forced to review their ingrained elitist biases. They, too, have to muster popular support once the incumbent government mounts a levée en masse (in the areas under its control) to resist the technically proficient yet narrowly based armed assault. However distasteful and risky this step may be for them, they cannot avoid it if they mean to persist in their bid for partial or total victory. As they cast about for recipes for mass mobilization, foreign counterrevolutionary regimes provide guidance by the sheer force of their living models.

Until such moments of unanticipated need traditional ruling

classes disdain and ignore embryonic counterrevolutionary leaders and movements. They assume that they have sufficient prestige, expertise, and resources to challenge vacillating governments and coalitions without putting on a "specious democratic mask." But once the thwarted pronunciamento turns into a confrontation of civil-war dimensions, the use-values of that mask become self-evident. The elites need soldiers, coercers, and avengers, and they need them quickly and in substantial numbers.

To hasten and facilitate the raising of these executioners of violence, the old cadres license counterrevolutionary leaders to generate the rousing appeals and provide the organizational weapons for mass mobilization and regimentation. This is the writ that transforms the limited pronunciamento into an ideologically charged crusade. Since such crusading is uncongenial to their style and temperament, the grandees arrange to have it done by proxy. But they never lose control of the counterrevolutionary movement that they call to life and harness to their cause: they provide the money, the secular legitimation, and the religious benison. In addition, the old guard is careful not to raise up a counterrevolutionary leader of independent charismatic force. The chief of the *pronunciadores* sees to it that he also remains the chief of the licensed counterrevolutionaries. The two chains of command come together in his person and office. And both of these remain a hard conservative-*cum*-reactionary core, protected, reinforced, and cloaked by layers of counterrevolutionary rhetoric, social carriers, and methods.

In other words, the counterrevolutionary movement is and remains an auxiliary instrument, manipulated by an intrinsically traditional yet outwardly ideological conservative leader. During and after the civil war, the authoritarian power of this leader is anchored in the army, backstopped by the subordinate counterrevolutionary movement. These two levers of coercive control enable him not only to preside over the upper cartel of anxiety, but also to be the ultimate arbiter of its intramural conflicts of interest and of influence. Landowners, industrialists, churchmen, and civil servants do not consider this imposed arbitration an excessive price to pay for the reconquest and maintenance of their social, class, and economic positions. The authoritarian arbiter may not be their obedient agent; but neither are they his pliant puppets. They need and use each other within the confines of a restorative project whose counterrevolutionary thrust remains half domant and half ceremonial in relatively normal times.

The _disguised counterrevolution_ accompanies a revolution from above. Internal cleavages and dislocations, usually aggravated by defeat in war or diplomacy, prompt or even force incumbent rulers and elites to renounce prerogatives and to grant concessions. These tend to be rigorously confined to the constitutional and legal spheres, though even these changes in public law may not go nearly as far as at first appears. Much depends on the extent to which top civil servants, military officers, and judges are replaced instantly; and on the extent to which the basis for their recruitment is broadened for the immediate future. If most of the critical posts remain in their hands, the revolution from above may never strike firm roots, the more so because, initially, it barely tears through the symbolic, religious, and economic fabric of polity and society.

In any case, many who sympathize with, support, and incite counterrevolution lurk among these seasoned civil, military, and legal cadres that stay on in the government. Moreover, these have close connections with fraternal, economic, and political associations, pressure groups, and cabals that are, or see themselves as, the prime losers of the officially ordained new deal. At first, key spokesmen of such groups urge outright repression of dissidents; then they insistently oppose concessions; and finally they grudgingly suffer what they denounce as a premature and unwarranted surrender.

Eventually these hard-liners in and out of government regroup their forces. Especially once the worst of the crisis is over and order is restored, they press not only for an instant end to all further capitulations, but also for the gradual restriction and preferably the outright cancellation of recent reform measures.

Meanwhile, the same conditions also activate outright counterrevolutionaries who until now may have been relatively quiescent. They organize and act on their own. But from the very outset they encounter a flexible mixture of patronage, protection, and instigation from sympathetic government cadres and from irreconcilable strata of the conservative-reactionary complex. Indeed, the extent and effectiveness of this sponsorship condition and possibly determine the scope and intensity of the counterrevolutionary impulse.

Because they are explicitly antideferential, counterrevolutionaries do not hesitate to strike out even while the revolution from above is in its most delicate phase. The conservatives who stage this operation would prefer not to have to keep an eye on their rear, being fully and dangerously engaged in containing the revolution out front. But this is the very moment that the counterrevolutionaries decide to make their presence felt: to threaten and carry out pogroms, political assassinations, and/or incursive forays against struggling minorities along or across outlying borders. They are determined to take advantage of the government's disarray and the security forces' preoccupation with revolutionary disorders; to test their strength, tactics, and sponsors; and to encourage outraged conservatives and reactionaries in and out of government to actively oppose the panic-inspired policy of cowardly accommodation.

Not that the transitional government as a whole welcomes this furtive counterrevolution. In fact, its members and advisers are severely divided over it. A few ministers and officials may actually threaten to resign unless the counterrevolutionary transgressors are promptly punished and bridled. But all the others either overlook, minimize, condone, or favor their excesses. Of course, it is perfectly understandable that in the disorder and tension of the times, newly appointed *political* officeholders should hesitate to order experienced officers, policemen, and magistrates of questionable loyalty to enforce order against those with whom they sympathize. Even ministers of even-handed disposition yield to the argument that nothing should be done to split and hence weaken the internal security agencies until after the revolutionary danger has been firmly checked. Also, they are susceptible to the warning that unless the army is kept intact further or future foreign-policy setbacks will be inevitable.

In any case, key members of the executive and judicial branches of government at the central, provincial, and local level surreptitiously cover the activities of counterrevolutionaries with mixes of personal, institutional, and official sanction. Intermittently they extend help in the form of symbolic gestures, special funds, police and military participation or protection, and judicial leniency. Once the situation is stabilized, the counterrevolutionary campaign subsides, and so does this government protection. By then the conservative and reactionary elements in and out of government have recovered their poise and many of their positions. They are confident that they have kept or regained the power and influence necessary to weather and, if need be, to curtail or disembody the recent constitutional readjustments.

Although they now disavow or dismiss counterrevolutionary helpers, they do not outlaw or surveil them nearly as rigorously as they do their revolutionary counterparts. In fact, the cadres that collaborated at the height of the crisis remain entrenched in the government, ready to resume this collaboration in any future emergency. Similarly, the upper cartel of anxiety maintains distant and often rival, but nevertheless nurtured relations with counterrevolutionary leaders. The latter neither can nor should be ignored as they proceed to build their movement in the streets, at the polls, and in the legislative chambers. With their growing bases of autonomous influence and power, counterrevolutionary leaders acquire the leverage which enables them to make a bid if not for supremacy or parity in the antirevolutionary triad, then certainly for a less humiliatingly subservient role.

Clearly, in initiating a revolution from above, the frightened but ultimately supple conservatives and reactionaries yield the form rather than the substance of power. This superstructural transfer of political positions to representatives of the center left, signified by constitutional changes, breaks the mushrooming yet brittle opposition bloc. It also enables the incumbent regime and elites to buy the continuation of their untrammeled control of bureaucracy, army, police, and judiciary. Needless to say, the designated ministers may make some marginal inroads into these vital preserves of state power. But they are unlikely to make any lasting dents, notably because for a variety of reasons they do not foster any of the social and economic forces and changes which would enable them to reduce their subservience to their constricting mentors.

Moreover, by agreeing to give first if not exclusive priority to the repression of revolutionary forces and disorders, the ministers take a turn that is certain to salvage and reinforce the failing regime. But in taking this turn they also become accomplices, in spite of themselves, in the legitimation of counterrevolutionary vanguards and experimentation in counterrevolutionary methods. The resulting thrust not only undermines their own power, prestige, and integrity, but it burdens their political rule with a stunting legacy: they can become neither their own masters nor the servants of those popular forces that originally frightened yesterday's rulers into taking a back seat, however temporarily.

The _anticipatory counterrevolution_ is engineered by ruling elites and cadres that have firm control of the government apparatus. They first foster a counterrevolutionary movement for their own purposes. But then they strike against it pre-emptively in order to avoid being excessively pressed, if not surpassed, by it. In the process, the incumbent power elite itself absorbs important aspects of the counterrevolutionary project, yet without cutting into the essence of its own power and authority.

Actually, the international situation provides the context for the anticipatory counterrevolution. The old ruling groups are stimulated to a pre-emptive strike from above against counterrevolutionaries by the unenviable fate of their counterparts in one or more other countries. They are the more determined to act in good time because these other countries encourage and support the indigenous counterrevolutionary movement from across the borders. This external aid is designed to undermine the power of the incumbent governors and their supporters and is also directed against the particular foreign policy on which the latter stake their own future.

Still, the counterrevolutionary movement could never have assumed threatening proportions without prior sponsorship from within the establishment, including from within the government. Its leaders needed the near-constant toleration and the intermittent help of the ruling class and its strategic elites in order to build their mass organization, stage their punitive raids or pogroms, and sustain their ambition for supreme power. All the while, they served their conservative and reactionary patrons by providing them with supplementary power for their battle against claimant middle classes, workers, and peasants.

The patrons and paymasters who foster the counterrevolutionary movement that eventually threatens even them are carriers and officials of essentially authoritarian governments. Military and bureaucratic cadres, usually, but not always, in conjunction with a royal chief and his camarilla, have learned to tighten their control by flaunting the specter of internal revolution. To the extent that this specter is ephemeral—and it usually is in repressive regimes—they claim that its real danger stems from its being subject to inflation and manipulation from across the border, where the world revolution has its headquarters.

When there is a renewed upswing in domestic tensions and foreign difficulties, the leaders of such conventional authoritarian systems have less to worry about from decimated revolutionary forces than from the dynamic counterrevolutionary movement that operates with their license. That movement is equipped and eager to exploit the dissatisfactions of the crisis strata and to enlist support from abroad, and it does so in preparation for a test of strength with its patrons. In the face of this acute danger, conservatives and reactionaries pull together. They also prevail on otherwise unfriendly center-rightists and center-leftists to support a pre-emptive coup. They do so with the disarming argument that such a course is the only effective antidote to full and extreme counterrevolution.

The incumbent government, which is authoritarian to begin with, becomes still more authoritarian in this flight into dictatorship. Whatever remains of civil, parliamentary, and judicial liberties is further curtailed as a part and consequence of the campaign against the militant counterrevolutionary movement. Since the primary aim is to destroy this movement's capacity for independent and disciplined action, the internal security forces move to arrest, exile, and, in some instances, execute its top leadership, and to dissolve its most fanatical terror units or military cliques.

Once decapitated, the movement ceases to be a threat to the time-honored ruling classes—political, economic, social, bureaucratic, military, and ecclesiastic. This being so, rather than destroy it altogether, they proceed to make it their own. Confronted with mounting popular restlessness, the old guard prefers to supplement conventional methods of police repression with controls of a newer vintage. Accordingly, having confirmed their primacy, the incumbent rulers and their supporters adopt a considerable range of counterrevolutionary methods. The chief executive—be he king, general, or civil servant—becomes a popular leader. He and some of his chief lieutenants adopt imitation salutes, uniforms, insignia, and slogans. Inflamed superpatriotism, usually combined with virulent anti-Semitism, becomes the preeminent note in their rhetoric. They emasculate or dissolve legislative chambers and rival parties. At the same time they launch a single or dominant party formation into which yesterday's auxiliary movement, minus its principal leaders, is absorbed.

In sum, the traditional authoritarian government is transmuted into a plebiscitary authoritarian regime controlled by and at the service of the upper cartel of anxiety. Within this regime, those counterrevolutionary elements that survive operate under the watchful eyes of military and police forces. But the latter are permeated by officers who, though loyal to the regime, nevertheless have strong counterrevolutionary affinities. As a result, behind the authoritarian regime's populist façade may be said to lurk latent but real counterrevolutionary impulses and forces, ready to strike whenever unleashed either by the government or by an intervening foreign power.

The international variable is of central importance not only in the anticipatory counterrevolution but also in the externally licensed and externally imposed varieties. In all three there is an intense interaction between two sets of factors: on the one hand, interlocked national conditions and indigenous counterrevolutionary developments and, on the other hand, equally interlocked diplomatic necessities and foreign counterrevolutionary influences. In each country, the course of events is a function of the degree to which security, economic, and political requirements further dependence on or reduce resistance to intervention by the foreign power that is the principal exponent and carrier of counterrevolution.

Needless to say, no government or regime, whatever its political coloration, voluntarily compromises its country's sovereignty, territorial integrity, and military security. Accordingly, when staging an anticipatory counterrevolution, the old rulers mean to increase their internal control in pursuit not only of self-serving class and status purposes but also of more effective diplomatic action. In some instances, foreign policy is calculated to minimize external losses, in others to maximize external gains. But whatever these instrumental diplomatic purposes, the ultimate aim is twofold: at one and the same time to use and to contain the counterrevolution, both nationally and internationally.

These two motions of anticipatory policy are not easily reconciled. Much depends on the will of the vanguard counterrevolutionary regime, whose probing foreign policy challenges the status quo and the procedural ground rules of the international order. In the last analysis, the power and needs of this necessarily expansionist regime determine the establishment of _externally licensed or externally imposed counterrevolutions_ in the defeated or satellite countries within its orbit.

Whenever a country faces military defeat, the victor power or powers define the terms of the political consequences of defeat. At first, in the face of serious reverses, the hard-pressed government broadens its political base by yielding or attributing cabinet and military posts to representatives of both the left and the right opposition. But before long, the influence of the attacking counterrevolutionary power tells in favor of the latter, particularly if these reverses quickly assume disastrous proportions.

The government that staggers along under such debilitating military blows not only lacks the time to organize a _levée en masse;_ it is also subject to political pressures, both domestic and foreign, which are ranged against any military policy that entails the strengthening of the center-left, let alone the strengthening of outright reformists and revolutionaries. Internally, the upper cartel of anxiety, including the military and bureaucratic castes, prefers a timely yet onerous negotiated settlement to the social and economic costs and risks of a protracted battle for a problematical victory. Alone indigenous counterrevolutionary leaders could conceivably provide the incumbent establishment and ruling classes with relatively safe popular carriers for a fight to the finish. But counterrevolutionaries are not about to mount the barricades to do battle against a foreign enemy for whom they have greater affinities than they have for most of their would-be coalition partners at home. Besides, unless there are paramilitary units in existence or on instant standby, the invading armies may not leave native counterrevolutionary leaders the time to forge the crisis strata into a people's militia. Precisely because any counterrevolutionary *levée en masse* cannot help but be explicitly sectarian and schismatic, its leaders find it more difficult to unchain latent enthusiasms in underlying populations than their revolutionary counterparts.

In addition, unless absolutely necessary, the aggressing counterrevolutionary power is careful not to encourage and brazenly affiliate with ideologically kindred elements in defeated or satellite nations. Although within their own country they settle for nothing less than first place in the political authority system, abroad these counterrevolutionary leaders prefer to leave traditional elites in control. If these elites can be counted on to collaborate, this indirect rule offers numerous advantages in all countries except those earmarked for outright annexation (rather than for satellite status).

To begin with, by taking over the government for the purpose of arranging a negotiated surrender, traditional elites save the victorious power the costs—military, economic, political—of a protracted struggle for total victory. While the conquering power is spared a military effort which it can promptly redirect into another phase of its foreign-policy project, the conservative governors of the vanquished nation salvage significant elements of sovereignty, territory, and economic riches. By seemingly wresting these concessions from the victor, they can ostentatiously claim that their essentially humiliating yet self-serving diplomatic course is an act of statesmanlike national salvation. But above all, the aggressing counterrevolutionaries from across the borders and the accommodating elites in the surrendering nation share a common minimal interest: they want to terminate military hostilities without the breakdown of vital services, the exasperation of war-weary soldiers and civilians, and the activation of revolutionary politicians who galvanize amorphous popular disaffection into purposeful political contestation.

After a military and diplomatic arrangement has been worked out, the two parties continue to serve one another. Lacking the resources to rule its expanding orbit directly, the preponderant counterrevolutionary regime is eager for collaborationist regimes to do its bidding. It therefore leaves these regimes with those attributes of sovereignty which enable them to strike an independent posture. They are licensed to control and run their countries with an indigenous bureaucracy, judiciary, army, and police. This licensed independence is designed to dissimulate the full extent of foreign counterrevolutionary control, domination, occupation, and/or exploitation, for which local conservatives and reactionaries are a convenient foil. Though this independence is more apparent than real, it does help to transform outright hostility into resignation mixed with hope.

To be sure, the major licensing power keeps a close watch. Should its foreign collaborators become too exigent, it can coerce them into continuing tractability by bringing superior military force into play; by withdrawing support for preferred territorial and trade positions; by fostering opposition among dissatisfied national, cultural, or sectional minorities; and, as a last resort, by unleashing native counterrevolutionary formations.

Though these potential and barely disguised sanctions do much to keep these licensed regimes in line, the fabric of mutual interests constitutes an even stronger bond for this marriage of convenience. The old-line classes and rulers, as well as their docile strategic elites, cannot seize, consolidate, or maintain power without foreign help. By themselves they are too weak to prevail against the center-left and its more radical supporters at the same time that they wish to check counterrevolutionary helpers and claimant minorities. In addition, to the extent that

their tenure is contingent on the successful implementation of a
certain foreign policy, they are at the mercy of the dominant
counterrevolutionary power. In other words, the intramural conflicts among reactionaries, conservatives, and counterrevolutionaries assume an international dimension: the old guards rely on
the intervention of the counterrevolutionary power from abroad
in order to survive without excessive concessions to their counterrevolutionary accomplices at home.

All along, however, these collaborationist efforts are rooted in
a counterrevolutionary matrix. Admittedly, most politically engaged collaborationists are not outright counterrevolutionaries.
Quite the contrary. They see and advertise themselves as the
most effective and least harmful prophylaxis against not only the
revolutionary but also the counterrevolutionary peril. Moreover,
reactionaries and conservatives collaborate with varying degrees
of enthusiasm, self-consciousness, and self-interest. Some are
moved by essentially political and ideological considerations;
others by calculations of material or social advancement. Many
men and women collaborate in relative innocence; still more do
so to avoid hardships or to secure petty preferments.

But whatever the nature and intensity of motive and purpose,
each collaborationist feeds into an intricate political amalgam
whose counterrevolutionary momentum, both national and international, is undeniable. Even political actors who claim to collaborate reluctantly, insisting that they do so only to avert the
worsening of their nation's domestic and international situation,
are tied into this complex. Besides, whether intentionally or unintentionally, these innocents first contributed to the constellation
of forces, both national and international, which launched the
counterrevolutionary juggernaut; and subsequently they collaborate without sacrifice of person, class, or status. Moreover,
at the same time that they allegedly bore from within in the
interest of the occupied or satellized commonweal, the old
guards, including the religious notables, condone the activities
of counterrevolutionaries and their fellow travelers at home and
abroad. They may not do so consciously or lightly. Nevertheless,
they do so—partly for political reinsurance, partly to please their
licensors, and partly out of habitual callousness toward the

plight of those less fortunate than themselves. Without this silent approval, not to say complicity, of these presumably self-less servants of the nation, collaborationists of avowed counter-revolutionary persuasion would find it that much more difficult to thrive within the licensed government and outside it.

In sum, military, landed, clerical, and bureaucratic elites, attended by expert notables on loan from the undisturbed industrial, commercial, and financial worlds, operate basically traditional autocratic or dictatorial authority systems. These old guards, usually but not always welded together by a royal personage, take advantage of the international conjuncture to re-establish or better their political and social sway without unduly encroaching on the nonpolitical and nonideological interests and prerogatives of confident capitalists, scientists, and clerks. The latter agree to renounce politics—to become unpolitical—in exchange for the preservation of their job, class, and status, for which they can continue to logroll with the upper cartel of anxiety. But anxious and self-assured grandees alike agree to pay the price of assimilating, fostering, or condoning the activities of counterrevolutionaries in and out of government.

As for the motives and purposes of outright counterrevolutionaries, they are as varied as those of the other varieties of collaborationists. Some are ideological fanatics, other ordinary opportunists, and still others calculating realists. The leaders divide into propagandists, organizers, commanders, and politicians. Among the rank and file there are profiteers, informers, terrorists, and torturers, as well as volunteers eager to fight the ostensibly revolutionary enemy on the home front and on foreign battlefields. On the whole, compared with their native sponsors and abettors, these counterrevolutionaries have a more modest social, class, and occupational profile and a less balanced psychological one. Not surprisingly, their profiles approximate those of their foreign models or intermittent foreign paymasters and directors, with due allowance for the overrepresentation of dissatisfied national, cultural, or sectional minorities.

In both occupied and satellized countries counterrevolutionary collaborationism plays a distinctly subordinate role as long as the modus vivendi works to the satisfaction of the licensor.

If these regimes nevertheless acquire a counterrevolutionary image, they do so less because of officially perpetrated or instigated excesses than as a result of the adoption of counter-revolutionary slogans, rituals, and gestures, and the toleration of counterrevolutionary leaders, formations, demonstrations, and publications.

But as soon as serious strains develop between the paramount power and its licensed regimes, the abeyant and restrained coun-terrevolutionary forces begin to assert or reassert themselves. Having overextended itself militarily and economically, this imperious power makes increasingly exacting demands. It re-quires greater tributes of food, raw materials, manufacturers, and manpower at the very time when worsening local conditions make their fulfillment intolerably burdensome.

Shortages of consumer goods, shrinking food rations, rising prices, forced labor, and mounting war casualties spark the re-sumption of the civil war, both national and international, that was recently interrupted by the successful establishment of dif-ferent variants of counterrevolutionary regimes. For a time, the revolutionary and reformist forces are either obliterated or in headlong retreat. In addition, their external supporters are in no position to furnish any aid except, at best, moral and ideologi-cal encouragement.

Presently, the lately expired and intensely loathed popular or united fronts revive in the form of resistance or guerrilla move-ments. Mounting privations and sacrifices spiked by despair about the future help swell their ranks. Simultaneously the promise and reality of foreign aid improve their prospects of success.

In other words, the vanguard counterrevolutionary regime fal-ters, and with it all the licensed regimes within its orbit. In the former, the subservient old-line elites set forth to capitalize on their political masters' difficulties. They do so in the hope of salvaging their class and social position, of improving their political hold, and of rehabilitating themselves in the eyes of their subjects. Not that they propose either a revolution or fundamental reforms. Rather, they wish a revolution from above in their own favor. They seek the restoration of the authority system that preceded the pre-emptive counterrevolution, modified to eliminate interference with elitist rule by plebiscitary pressures from the right and equalitarian pressures from the left. Chastened by their experience with counterrevolutionary "helpers" who manipulate interstitial crisis strata, and as determined as ever to contain all reformists and revolutionaries, these reactionary and conservative grandees prefer to operate—and have to operate—without a popular base. Their chances for survival, exoneration, and success depend almost entirely on developments outside their own country, notably on the course of the resumed international civil war. They know that sooner or later the antirevolutionary side in that overarching conflict will appreciate their worth: in exchange for their stabilizing services the old-line elites will be allowed and helped to save their honor, status, and wealth even if their congealed political formulas are spurned.

Meanwhile, within the occupied and satellized countries the situation is altogether different. There old-line elites are in power, while native counterrevolutionaries are poised to take advantage of their plight. The licensed rulers wind up being beset on all sides. In their rear they face mounting resistance or guerrilla movements. These refuse to differentiate between traditional elites and their counterrevolutionary helpers, insisting that the two, though not cut of identical cloth, nevertheless need each other to survive. Spurning the elite's argument of the lesser evil, insurgents attack all segments of the counterrevolutionary triad with equal force.

In front of them the licensed regimes face defeat in war. Naturally, the advancing enemy plans to secure territorial readjustments and financial reparations. More ominous, however, is the enemy's determination not to settle for a surface reshuffling of government personnel but to insist on a change in regime.

Simultaneously, above them, the besieged governors are subject to intensifying pressures from their licensors, whose own difficulties make them doubly oppressive. The paramount power means to enforce compliance with its ukases for higher tribute and unwavering solidarity. As a last resort, it intervenes to establish an externally imposed counterrevolutionary regime.

This prospect of external intervention encourages native counterrevolutionaries to press their sponsoring elites for an enlarged scope for their paramilitary and terrorist activities, as well as for a greater voice in government and administration. These counterrevolutionary leaders and activists, most of them heavily committed and compromised, realize that hereafter their fortunes are tied irrevocably to those of their external sponsors. At a minimum, the vanguard power's position must be secured. This is the essential prerequisite for the preservation of a world political orbit in which licensed regimes can continue to function and to keep counterrevolutionary leaders and formations on tap, if not on top. From a more hopeful and bolder perspective, counterrevolutionary leaders of occupied or satellized countries look ahead to full control under the umbrella of a solidly implanted counterrevolutionary center. To achieve either one of these goals, they are prepared to compromise their nation's territorial, economic, and moral patrimony while at the same time mobilizing a *levée en masse* of such segments of the crisis strata as can still be frightened into an all-or-nothing stand.

The resurgence of internal revolutionary and reformist forces, reinforced by sympathetic impulses from abroad, enables counterrevolutionaries to once again flaunt the specter of revolution. To the extent that there is no centrist bloc for the old guard to resurrect and hide behind, and to the extent that the advancing enemy armies are carriers of a revolutionary project, to that extent counterrevolutionaries are likely to make headway.

Not surprisingly, this multiple squeeze aggravates the usual intramural rivalries among the major factions and supporting interest groups of the licensed government. In this crisis all alike, collectively and individually, must once again review their relationship with counterrevolutionary elements at home and abroad, in the government and outside. Is this a time to reduce, maintain, or increase collaboration with them? In answering this question, individuals and factions consult their conscience while also making a careful interest, class, social, and political calculation. Inevitably, the course of the international civil war vitally affects these deliberations and calculations.

Eventually, the military needs of the vanguard counterrevolutionary power decide this issue. Its troops advance at the same time that counterrevolutionaries who were kept on tap either locally or across the border are unleashed. A counterrevolutionary regime is installed with bayonets, though the deposed elites tend to be treated leniently. This externally imposed regime is charged with organizing the satellized or occupied country to fight more loyally, effectively, and fiercely than its hesitant and recalcitrant predecessor. In fact, it now mounts a sectarian and forced *levée en masse* to do battle in a conflict that has become as much a civil as an international war.

In the final analysis, then, counterrevolution is a sectarian *levée en masse within* unstable but legitimate authority systems, *with* the complicity of frightened reactionaries and conservatives, *against* massive enemies at home and abroad, and *for* the monopolistic control of state and government by a new political elite. Any such *levée en masse* requires a supreme leader; needs stirring propaganda appeals; is regimented by new cadres; develops an internal camaraderie with equalitarian overtones; and displays an élan that is characteristic of embattled communities of either old or new believers.

Counterrevolutions, whatever their variety, are less historically creative than revolutions. The ideologies of counterrevolutionary movements and regimes are solidly anchored in venerated principles, values, attitudes, and habits, both secular and religious, of established societies; their social carriers come from strata that have already climbed beyond the first rungs of the social, professional, and income ladder; their programs call for the purification rather than transformation or overthrow of existing institutions; and their political allies are recruited from incumbent power and ruling elites. In addition to these ill-concealed ties to the past and present, counterrevolutionary ideologists and leaders imitate and simulate, but do not copy, some of the stylistic and programmatic features of the hated revolutionary rival. Still, these elements of continuity, contrivance, and imitation notwithstanding, counterrevolutionary movements and regimes have a distinctiveness and wholeness of their own. Their project is meant to create the impression that they seek fundamental changes in government, society, and community. In reality their blueprints and policies are at best pseudo-revolutionary.

This much seems clear as well: at every step counterrevolutionaries are rigorously enmeshed with all varieties of reactionaries and conservatives. Regardless of who dismisses or controls whom, these three distinct factions of the antirevolutionary triad need, use, and ultimately spare each other. To be sure, their co-operation is strained by strong and persistent ideological frictions, personal rivalries, conflicts of interest, and social antagonisms. In addition, their relations are punctuated by mutual suspicion, slander, disdain, and recrimination. But in spite of all these tensions and conflicts, reactionaries, conservatives, and counterrevolutionaries cling to each other. And in the event that they have a falling out, with rare exceptions the faction or factions that carry the day stop short of purging their partners. Temporary imprisonment or exile tends to be the worst fate for the leaders of those factions that are forced from a dominant, or coordinate, to a subordinate place. Because, after all, reactionaries, conservatives, and counterrevolutionaries never know when they will need to use each other again.

Meanwhile, the superordinate economic, military, bureaucratic, religious, and social institutions and cadres continue essentially undisturbed. Together with the reactionary and conservative political class, they will survive the defeat or abandonment of the counterrevolutionary project unless external forces combine with internal insurgents to sweep them away.

part three

Questions

5. Research Design: Counterrevolution

The form and intensity of counterrevolutionary movements and regimes are a function of the structural conditions and conjunctural developments, national and international, that impinge upon them.

In an era of historical turbulence, each country has a counter-revolutionary potential with distinct regional and local variations. This potential is rooted in arrested, ailing, neglected, or artificially bolstered economic sectors, geographic areas, and cultural minorities. These call for preliminary analysis because they provide a reservoir of dormant economic, social, and political carriers and directors of counterrevolution. Specifically, at the grass roots they harbor marginal farmers, small shopkeepers, self-employed artisans, underemployed professionals, frozen white collar workers, and underpaid civil servants. At another level there are agricultural, industrial, and commercial sectors whose privileged survival or advancement, also in social terms, depend on government subsidies, tariffs, and contracts.

Even before any major storms break, both the latent popular crisis strata and quiescent segments of an upper cartel of anxiety express themselves through distinct lobbies, interest associations, pressure groups, and political parties. Moreover, nervous elites, usually advised and represented by premature counter-revolutionaries, begin to forge organizational links between themselves and certain lower centers or sectors of lingering dissatisfaction.

Sudden and acute economic, diplomatic, and military exigencies—in varying combinations—actuate, swell, and galvanize these vulnerable strata and their organizations. In particular, economic vicissitudes aggravate not only their material conditions and prospects but also their psychological distempers. Both require close analysis. Of course, the categories, methods, and data for the aggregate and individual measurement of the

119

former are far superior to those available for the examination of the latter. Even so, every effort must be made to probe the strength or weakness of the correlations between changing economic fortunes on the one hand and subjective indentifications, ideational persuasions, and, above all, political actions on the other.

This correlational analysis is indispensable for the explication and understanding of the behavior and conduct of incumbent power, ruling, and strategic elites. Apart from the fact that there are written sources from which to attempt a reconstruction of their inner springs of action, in times of stress they become critical weathervanes and pacesetters. In the face of real or putative revolutionary dangers, they provide much of the legitimation for the advancing politics of anxiety, alienation, and fear.

Needless to say, intense conjunctural exigencies stimulate not only latent counterrevolutionary forces but also their revolutionary opposites. The result is the double-edged crisis in which both revolutionary and counterrevolutionary leaders exploit and contribute to the decomposition of polity, economy, and society; the growth of extraconsensual ideas and politics; and the erosion of the vital stabilizing center.

But whereas the revolutionary project aims at a total transcendence, the counterrevolutionary project has a much more limited scope: the transformation of the polity for the purpose of restabilizing and maintaining the economy and society. In any such preservative scheme the role of reactionary and conservative forces and leaders is pivotal.

In this research design the emphasis falls squarely on developments within the antirevolutionary rather than within the revolutionary camp. Not that the revolutionary side of the Janus-faced crisis should be ignored altogether. But its internal composition and dynamics can be slighted in favor of attention to its external vectors. In particular, light should be thrown on the attitudes and actions toward the antirevolutionary triad on the part of revolutionary actors and theorists.

But more consequential still are the views of the revolutionary side held by reactionaries, conservatives, and counterrevolutionaries. To understand the counterrevolutionary phenomenon it is far more important to discern the mutations of hostile perceptions and evaluations of revolutionary capabilities, intentions, and acts than to reconstruct their objective realities. At critical points, incumbent elites in and out of government are moved to condone, support, or implement counterrevolutionary policies, either by genuine (but not necessarily objectively justified) fear or by calculations of disguised expediency.

Clearly, this construct assigns substantive and analytic priority to the interaction of infrastructural conditions with conjunctural events and to its refraction by politically engaged incumbent elites. Accordingly, it takes exception to the depolitization of crisis politics that continues to be so fashionable in scholarly and intellectual circles. This depolitization often takes the form of substituting psychologically informed biographical and intellectual history for the contextual study of intertwined group and ideational conflicts.

Almost invariably, biographers attribute the behavior and conduct of counterrevolutionary political actors to psychological and mental deviancies which are only remotely and marginally conditioned by larger environmental factors. Similarly, historians of the growth of counterrevolutionary ideas tend to ascribe not just the philosophic inconsistencies but even the central significance of these ideas to the neurotic personality, social malaise, and political innocence of the intellectuals that conceive them.

But surely, no matter how sophisticated, this psychological reductionism invites skepticism. At a minimum, biographical and intellectual historians still have to develop sound and convincing distinctions between strictly psychological, psychologically relevant, and psychologically conditioned factors. In the meantime, the psychological components, not to say determinants of individual political action and intellection can be only an ancillary, and not a central, focus or explanatory postulate for an inquiry such as this.

In any case, this construct presumes that whatever their psychological motives, directors of counterrevolutionary thought and action, as well as their reactionary and conservative associates, act and think in functionally rational ways. It proposes careful scrutiny of the extent to which instrumental calculations --which can turn out to be miscalculations—guide them not only in the promotion of their respective interests but also in the search for psychological gratifications.

Besides, each individual's twofold quest for advantage and gratification is significantly conditioned by elements of social, economic, cultural, and political commonality. Motivational as well as objective mainsprings of action are modified by group membership and behavior. It is as risky to extrapolate from the behavior of an isolated individual to that of a group as it is to analogize from the dynamics of *intra*group behavior and action to that of *inter*group relations.

It would appear that in times of crisis the motivational components of individual and collective action are more pressing in the different layers of the crisis strata than in either the upper cartel of anxiety or the upper echelons of counterrevolutionary movements. Both groups tend to vest leadership in individuals who manage to keep cool and calculating heads under conditions of acute stress.

Such leaders are nevertheless sensitive to the passions and attitudes that in moments of heightened disaggregation swell up among underlying and interstitial populations. They also realize that in the contemporary era these motivational components do not long remain spontaneous mainsprings of random action. Political leaders rush to incite, mobilize, structure, and direct them. Incumbent ruling elites may be reluctant to play on the fears, frustrations, prejudices, and aggressive impulses of the crisis strata. But they never really exhaust themselves to restrain counterrevolutionary leaders from harnessing these impulses, provided they channel such aggressive and destructive feelings against targets and for purposes that old elites consider compatible with their own projects.

It is in this process of mobilization that counterrevolutionary ideas assume their importance. They are neither an instant mix nor a magic wand. They have their own development and distinctive style. But these inner aspects ought not to be studied without constant reference to their external life, in which they take the form of ideology, doctrine, and program. In that form they speak to real issues. They also reach diverse audiences and serve political actors. From this larger perspective the personality and intent of an individual man of ideas is of secondary importance, and so are the intrinsic mediocrity and inconsistency of his thought.

Whatever their background characteristics and their motives, intellectual progenitors matter only to the extent that their ideas strike responsive chords. Novel aspects of their message are singled out for comment by book reviewers, editorialists, and publicists. Explicit references or subtle allusions show up in sermons, plays, novels, and poems. From the point of view of exciting interest in the nascent dispensation, critical and satirical comments, also by humorists and cartoonists, may well be as telling as approving ones. It is this preliminary dissemination and permeation that calls for careful examination, with close attention to the context and time when political actors weigh in.

They are the ones to speed up the incipient diffusion of proto-counterrevolutionary ideas. It would be instructive to have a collective profile of those politicians who wittingly initiate the appropriation and adaptation of such ideas for partisan ends; and to secure in-depth pictures of the local circumstances that prompt them to do so. Politicians distill clusters of general ideas and sentiments into phrases and slogans. These are designed to affect the motivational and objective needs of a variety of publics. Some appeals are shaped to exploit grievances and arouse hostilities in the crisis strata; others are formulated to dispel or reduce suspicions in the upper cartel of anxiety; still others are formed to quicken the growth of a shared perspective. Though discrete appeals carry messages geared to segmental predispositions and susceptibilities, they remain enveloped in the broader, unfolding ideology and doctrine from which they spring. This politicization of ideas—many of which are cultural, moral, and aesthetic—is filtered through a variety of media, each of which imposes its own thematic and stylistic demands.

It becomes increasingly easy to study the changing nature, intensity, and radius of this politicization once it assumes concrete organizational forms. The new outlook and formula begin to resonate through literary, cultural, religious, and fraternal societies; through interest and political associations; and through a separate daily, weekly, and periodical press.

All of these call for intensive examination, to be carried out with standard questions, methods, and tools, including group prosopography. Such quasi-monographic probes should be designed to provide a wide range of topically structured information: date and place of origin; profile and purposes of founding fathers; collective profile of top executive and administrative cadres; group physiognomy of committed, regular, and occasional members (readers); sources of finance; ideological, doctrinal, and/or programmatic posture; activities, schisms, and fusions; interlocking directors, paymasters, and members with other organizations. Obviously, factual tabulations must register secular mutations, conjunctural jolts, and variations due to local, regional, religious, and cultural factors.

But no matter how finely structured, such an inventory provides no more than raw data about the internal composition and life of early organized carriers of defection. Without further analysis, these factual representations, even if artfully interwoven, say little about their historical significance. The data must be pressed for clues to the external ties and impact of this secession. In particular, it should help to establish the secessionists' place, contacts, and sympathizers in the power, ruling, and strategic elites. In turn, they should provide tracers of the sensitivity, not to say responses, to the secession in reactionary and conservative parties; in the government, bureaucracy, and army; and in the churches.

Outright counterrevolutionary movements as well as their auxiliary and fellow traveling organizations must be subjected to even more rigorous scrutiny. The study of the physiognomy of the ascendant counterelite should reveal the differential characteristics of political leaders, propagandists, organizers, administrators, and coercers. Refinements should also sharpen the social profile of the rank and file. Even the effort to set apart flaming militants, confirmed activists, devoted members, dutiful followers, and sometime sympathizers forces attention to the motives and purposes behind varying intensities of commitment. Different segments of the crisis strata have different sorts and degrees of predispositions and susceptibilities to anxiety politics. Once set adrift by pressing conjunctures, each segment responds to a distinct admixture of appeals.

This is the point at which to strive for a calibrated approximation of the malleability of counterrevolutionary ideas and of the expediency with which they are manipulated. It would appear that this peremptory pragmatism is least pronounced when it comes to general ideological and doctrinal prescriptions. These provide myths and principles with which to justify concrete programmatic platforms. At the same time, they reflect and foster a climate of opinion that furthers attention to and receptivity of segmental appeals. In fact, specific promises and inducements, however varied and inconsistent, are imbedded in this ideology and doctrine, which lend themselves to rhetorical articulation and ritualistic incantation. What, then, are the dominant ideological and doctrinal themes, and which of them achieve and maintain greatest constancy in each of the major phases of political mobilization?

To answer these questions it is necessary to make detailed studies of political campaigning, not so much on the national as on the local and regional level. It is only natural that when addressing the national arena—in speech, in writing, on film—counterrevolutionary propagandists should expound their most general ideological, doctrinal, and even programmatic formulas. On such occasions the aim is to appeal to the entire spectrum of potential supporters; to avoid offense to or alignment with any one group; and to feed a febrile atmosphere and mood.

In less general and exposed settings counterrevolutionary spokesmen face a totally different challenge. There they need to win and hold recruits, followers, sympathizers, and patrons whose interests, grievances, doubts, and anxieties are segmentally conditioned. When compaigning they face particular audiences for which they formulate subappeals. These take careful account of patently felt economic, social, religious, ethnic, regional, and local needs, aspirations, and anxieties. In other words, discrete circumstances precipitate changing admixtures of abstract ideational and concrete programmatic formulas. A comparative study of municipal and regional campaigns alone—supported where relevant by an analysis of voting behavior—can help distinguish the ideological and doctrinal constants from the mundane variables in the counterrevolutionary project. These constants may also be reflected in and promoted by flags, insignia, uniforms, songs, festivals, and patron saints.

Because of sparse and doctored records, the reconstruction of the finances of counterrevolutionary movements is fraught with difficulties. In probing the internal sources of income it may be useful to distinguish membership dues; admissions and collections at meetings or rallies; and the sale of newspapers and pamphlets. Larger voluntary contributions can come from individuals, business firms, interest associations, government authorities, and foreign supporters. Individual contributors should be broken down into businessmen, landowners, salaried managers, and professionals. Once indentified, there is the further question as to whether individual donors as well as collective paymasters are tied into the upper cartel of anxiety or into otherwise steadfast segments of economy and society. As for concealed government subsidies, their fountainhead must be traced to the royal entourage, the interior ministry, or to special security branches.

Internal financial resources tend to correlate with membership figures and the scale of public activities. But the contributions of substantial individual and collective donors, including home and foreign governments, are much more likely to fluctuate with conjunctural developments and needs. Such paymasters do not expect their affiliation with the counterrevolutionary movement, which they keep secret, to advance their status and prestige. Rather, calculations of political and class interest move them to pay tribute. They seek to encourage and benefit from certain activities; to extract programmatic concessions; to exercise a restraining influence; or to hedge partisan bets.

These paymasters invite attention to the movement's multiple contacts—national, regional, local—with influential elites in government, in neighboring parties, in the cartel of anxiety, and in the establishment at large. These contacts vary in extent, intensity, and openness, and many of their consequences may be larger than intended. Some individuals take out membership cards, perhaps in auxiliary or fellow traveling rather than parent organizations. Government officials cannot and need not go that far. Magistrates, judges, and law-enforcement officers can further the cause through a sympathetic exercise of their functions. Moreover, together with a vast array of other grandees, including churchmen, they can make symbolic gestures: their conspicuous attendance at rallies and their social fraternizing can have considerable legitimizing force.

Each nation has its own pattern of indulgence, complicity, and restraint with regard to counterrevolutionary movements and actions. No such pattern is constant. It changes with conjunctures that undermine the stability of an incumbent government: economic crisis intertwined with political unrest and international complications. Especially if its life depends on political parties or factions that condone the counterrevolutionary enterprise, a government may find its ability to suppress the politics of the streets gravely impaired. In such situations the loyalty of army and police commanders becomes critical. If they lean toward indulgence and complicity, a policy of restraint becomes considerably more difficult.

Individual conjunctures must be approached with the conventional questions and tools of narrative political history. It is in specific historical situations that discrete political actors make compromises and alliances that have a certain logic of their own. To be sure, these actors and their institutional bases have concrete socioeconomic roots, and these should never be lost sight of. But by itself, the socioeconomic composition of the leaders and members of a national political organization does not explain its larger purposes and functions. In no small measure, these are defined by dominant political personalities. Although such political actors cannot afford to disregard these socioeconomic constraints altogether, they nevertheless claim and secure the discretion to shape policy and make decisions. Needless to say, the more elitist or authoritarian the ideology and structure of political organizations, the greater this leeway.

In the double-edged crisis, the political formations of the antirevolutionary side tend to be of the sort that leave their leaders exceptionally ample scope. As a result, these leaders can move swiftly and without excessive worry about being disavowed by their second echelon and followers. This is a precious advantage in moments of political impasse and governmental paralysis, notably in multiparty parliamentary systems. Precisely because antirevolutionary leaders have such great latitude, the historical reconstruction of critical turning points must concentrate heavily on their actions.

The different varieties of counterrevolution are not made by these leaders, but they are precipitated, launched, and directed by them. The motives and purposes behind their decisions are a microcosmic reflection of the mainsprings and nature of counterrevolution. And the decisions themselves are a good barometer of the changing relationship between forces within the antirevolutionary consortium. The decisions also reveal the appraisals made by reactionaries, conservatives, and counterrevolutionaries of the larger political constellation, both national and international, in which they have worked out their expedient accommodations.

The place of terror and war in this politics of mutual accommodation remains to be explored. Counterrevolutionaries not only mean to persuade and to induce; they are also prepared to coerce. White terror is an integral part of their project. It is used to intimidate individuals and groups into yielding, accommodating themselves, and abandoning all resistance. Fear does its work within the movement as well as outside. Terror has a distinct place in different phases of each of the varieties of counterrevolution: during the ascendant struggle for influence and power; following accession to power; in civil war; in the wake of "liberation"; and in the last-ditch battle for survival.

Among the coercers it is possible to distinguish directors, executioners, and rationalizers. The directors of white terror define the over-all goals, formulate the basic strategy, select the general targets, stipulate the methods, and supervise the execution. Some circumstances encourage individual terrorists to commit spontaneous and indiscriminate acts of brutality. Eventually, however, even these tend to become absorbed into a campaign of violence that is systematic, controlled, and aimed. Such a campaign is willfully implemented by the lieutenants, sergeants, and raw recruits of coercion. One might ask what their group physiognomy is, including their psychological profile. What differences are there between those who strike to kill, those who manhandle persons, and those who despoil property? By whom and how are specific victims pinpointed?

The justifiers of coercion, whether self-appointed or instructed, gear their explanations to different audiences. Some specialize in addressing reluctant collaborators; others in impressing would-be resisters; and still others in speaking to adherents of varying degrees of commitment. Needless to say this information about the terrorists serves to delineate only one side of the white terror. To get at the other side there is need for an equally systematic examination of the terror's victims, targets, and methods.

However, no matter how comprehensive and meticulously shaded, these statistical data about the white terror cannot speak for themselves. In times of political turmoil the objective realities of this terror—which can only be reconstructed retrospectively—count for less than their perception, estimate, and discussion by contemporaries. Even in those instances in which the essential "facts" about terrorist acts are essentially incontrovertible, in the heat of crisis politics they are distorted by all sides—except, perhaps, by the waning vital center—for partisan and agitational purposes.

In the inquiry that is proposed here, the analytic weight should fall principally on the changing attitude and behavior to the white terror of reactionary and conservative collaborationists, both actual and potential. What are the concrete circumstances and considerations that prompt such different degrees of complicity as sufferance, condonence, encouragement, support, and incitement? How do collaborationists justify their complicity to themselves, in inner circles, and publicly?

Perhaps easiest to discern are the reactions and actions of prominent political actors in royal households, cabinets, legislatures, and parties. Top-level bureaucrats, judges, police chiefs, and military officers should not be that much harder to check into. Depending on the authority system, cabinets and legislatures exercise different degrees of control over these high officials. Constitutional provisions and traditions affect not only their behavior but also that of lesser officials at all levels of government.

A searching diagnosis of official behavior in the face of mounting and concrete acts of white terror is long overdue. Perhaps it should begin at the periphery and only then turn to the centers of national power. How do local officials react to assaults on life and property? In the event that they are forewarned of an impending action, do they take any precautionary measures? Because the role of law-enforcement agencies is critical, their performance calls for exceptionally rigorous analysis. By social origin, status, function, and psychological set, policemen of all ranks are more predisposed to sympathize with the social carriers and purposes of white terror than of red terror. Some of them are precocious fellow travelers or adherents of counterrevolutionary movements, possibly even of their paramilitary arm. As a result, even assuming that a municipal or regional government resolves to steer an imparital course, it may lack the power to follow it. How, then, do policemen in and out of uniform act? And, in the event that local military garrisons are summoned to help, what is the bearing of their officers and men?

This probe of official reactions should be supplemented by a study of reactions in the community at large. The conduct of social institutions and strata toward the victims of terrorist activities may be the most sensitive of all barometers. Do hospitals provide medical services? Do universities and churches offer asylum and shelter? Do paramilitary units of revolutionary movements come to the defense of threatened victims? Do doctors and lawyers volunteer their services? And what about the sermons of local men of god, editorials of local newspapers, and declarations of local intellectuals and artists?

There is the further question as to how all concerned behave once an assassination, pogrom, or raid is over. Does the mayor or governing body press for vigorous investigations and legal prosecution? Do magistrates and judges obstruct this process altogether or impose lenient if not perfunctory sentences? There is the additional possibility that coercers who wind up in jail can count on jail wardens to connive in their escape.

But there is a larger question still: how do higher political, administrative, and legal authorities, particularly at the center, deal with subordinate officials who fail or refuse to exercise their functions correctly because of ideological affinities? It matters enormously whether such officials are reprimanded, demoted, or dismissed; or whether they are shielded, ostentatiously commended, or even promoted. Of course, the broader constellation of power determines which of these two tendencies is or becomes dominant. The positions of reactionary and conservative leaders, political formations, interest associations, and newspapers are likely to weigh heavily in the balance, as will that of religious notables. If the most important among all these ignore, minimize, or condone this complicity, counterrevolutionaries feel doubly encouraged to assign high priority to using and expanding their government beachheads.

This is not to say that the white terror ceases to complicate the forging or maintenance of effective cooperative links within the antirevolutionary triad. The issue of the white terror never stops inflaming endemic intramural rivalries and conflicts, even after particular accommodations have been made. Only outright counterrevolutionaries and sworn collaborationists consider terror an integral part of the operational code of crisis rule. All other team members feel uncomfortable. The question arises, therefore, as to the conditions that eventually stimulate some of them if not to explicitly protest the white terror, to nevertheless make conscious and deliberate efforts to curb it. Which of the terror's methods and victims do the upper strata become most exercised about, and how do they go about expressing their opposition?

Whereas the white terror embarrasses and irritates cooperation within the consortium, a forward foreign policy fosters it. Inflamed ultra-nationalism is a cementing force in that it is central not only to the ideology and value system of counterrevolutionaries but to that of all varieties of reactionaries and conservatives as well. Also, almost invariably all three are strongly predisposed to use external belligerency as a safety valve for mounting internal tensions.

At first, the stress falls heavily on the importance of eliminating internal divisions as a precondition for more effective diplomatic action. To the extent that this policy promises and produces a political truce and fusion at the expense of revolutionary, reformist, or even liberalizing forces, the old elites cooperate and rally with enthusiasm.

Following the breakthrough of a pre-emptive, anticipatory, or disguised counterrevolution, all is well until there are indications that the policy of fusion, reinforced by terror and preliminary rearmament, fails in its purpose. Grave economic and social problems that had subsided momentarily, once again stimulate pressures for infrastructural reforms, also in the populist wing of the counterrevolutionary movement.

This is the conjuncture that needs rigorous study to determine the degree to which the resurgence of internal stress affects the turn to heightened external belligerency or war. How do the influential leaders of the major factions and groups view the reopening of politically dangerous economic and social sores? Do any of them explicitly refer to the nexus of domestic and foreign policy? What remedial policies do they propose? Which of them advocate the transmutation of internal frustrations and conflicts into external ones? In answering this last question it is important to note the different motives and purposes that actuate officials in key positions in and out of government. Do these differ according to their socioeconomic roots, functional positions, and political persuasions? Old-line bureaucrats, officers, and grandees may be moved by an atavistically infused national and military ethos; businessmen by the search for cost-plus contracts and expanding foreign economic horizons; and spokesmen for underlying socioeconomic strata by the quest for steady income and employment in a war economy. These divergent but not mutually incompatible reasons are informed by a common fear of fundamental socioeconomic change. At the same time, and perhaps paradoxically, they may also reflect the wistful hope of certain circles to trade off the white terror for foreign war.

Do the principal counterrevolutionary leaders realize that a belligerent foreign policy has multiple attractions for their subordinate associates? Who are the ones to argue that a flight into diplomatic brinkmanship and war is the most expedient way to bridge over internal contradictions and, in the bargain, to maintain or strengthen their political rule in state and party? In other words, the fragile consortium is to be held together not only by a common fear of renewed internal disorders but also by the shared belief in an external mission.

Needless to say, this prescription to use foreign policy for purposes of domestic stabilization is contingent upon military and diplomatic possibilities. For it to be seriously advanced and considered within the consortium, it must not be out of line with the nation's warmaking capabilities and potentials. However, the international constellation of power must not foreclose the success of the first forays of this externalization of counterrevolution.

Much depends on developments within the major powers, as well as within the countries that are singled out as victims of diversionary assault. External counterrevolutionary probes take place in a time of universal unrest that makes cabinet diplomacy singularly difficult. Each government's foreign policy is subjected to intensely conflicting internal pressures. The advocates of the diversionary strategy do not create the internal political battles that buffet the major powers' external policies. But they do propose to exploit them for their own purposes. In particular, they mean to strengthen the hand of sympathetic political forces that recognize the international nature of the double-edged crisis.

At home, the specter of revolution frightens reactionaries and conservatives into condoning the white terror. That same specter is now manipulated to intimidate favorably disposed conservative and reactionary forces in other countries to appease diversionary foreign policy maneuvers. It is this cross-national dimension of the dynamics of foreign policy in an era of international civil war that still needs study. Each country gets caught up in a situation, both national and international, in which issues of foreign policy become first and foremost issues of domestic politics.

6. Internal Causes and Purposes of War in Europe, 1870–1956

When studying the motives and causes for war it is fashionable to focus on the aggressive drives of modern man, those same drives which are said to feed nonviolent forms of conflict, such as competition, opposition, and rivalry. One of the attractions of this approach is the implied prospect of banishing war in one of two ways: by restructuring society so as to reduce, if not eliminate, individual aggression, or by rechanneling man's bedrock of aggressiveness into socially sanctioned but harmless "aggression-absorbing" activities.[1] Incidentally, to date no one seems to have established any solid correlations—positive or negative—between the degree of aggressiveness of specific political actors, classes, or peoples and their disposition first to advocate war and then to shoulder its burdens.

In another analytic scheme, which is almost equally fashionable, the focus is on the harsh realities of international life in a world of multiple sovereign states, each state being bent on jealously guarding and enhancing its own independence and welfare under conditions of international anarchy. By implication this second focus makes the achievement of perpetual peace contingent on the contraction or disappearance of sovereignty as such.[2]

[1] See Konrad Lorenz, *On Aggression* (New York, 1967); and Jerome D. Frank, *Sanity and Survival: Psychological Aspects of War and Peace* (New York, 1968).

[2] See Hans Morgenthau, *Politics Among Nations*, 4th ed. (New York, 1967). For an anthropo-psychological interpretation of the mainsprings of this international conflict see Robert Ardrey, *The Territorial Imperative* (Boulder, Colo., 1966).

This paper was published originally in *The Journal of Modern History*, vol. 41, no. 3 (September 1969), pp. 291–303.

Admittedly both of these approaches have their merits. But they also have one flaw in common: both neglect or misjudge the vital political core of the decision to go to war. That decision is made by political actors and classes who in critical moments look at the dual field of domestic and international politics. When having recourse to war, these actors and classes conceive of it as an instrument of policy which, whether used successfully or unsuccessfully, produces important internal as well as external results. They anticipate that these domestic and foreign policy results will be of varying mixes, in terms both of their relations to each other and of their degrees of intentionality.

Another reason why, in critical moments, political actors carefully scrutinize the domestic side of war is that, compared with other forms of conflict, war is a distinctly collective phenomenon.[3] It is distinguished by conscious cooperation among and within all major segments of society. This being so, those facing the decision and responsibility for war are bound to weigh the degree of actual and potential loyalty and support among classes and masses alike. They make this evaluation not only for their own country and its allies but also for potential enemy nations, particularly under conditions of mass politics and in revolutionary eras.

At first glance Carl von Clausewitz seems altogether oblivious to the domestic causes, uses, and consequences of war. But a closer look at his work—which focuses so heavily on the impact of the new politics of the French Revolution on warfare—shows that his conception of war as a political act and instrument points squarely in this direction. For Clausewitz war "has its roots in a set of political circumstances" and is brought about "only by a political *Motiv*."[4] Given these very real political roots and impulses, war cannot be "an isolated act, that explodes suddenly and with complete surprise." The internal as well as the diplomatic preparations for war are part of its originating matrix,

---

[3] Gaston Bouthoul, *Les Guerres* (Paris, 1951), pp. 26–31.
[4] This and all subsequent quotations from Clausewitz are cited from his classic *Vom Kriege* (Berlin, 1957), pp. 22–25, 30–35, 726–35.

while its political purpose and intent fix the parameters of the aims to be achieved and the efforts to be expended. According to Clausewitz, this preparation, purpose, and design are decided and implemented not by abstract states but by governments composed of specific persons and acting under concrete historical conditions. Moreover, since the political purpose of war has to stimulate the masses to effort and sacrifice, this purpose must be so defined as to inspire a positive popular response.

In other words, the decision for and the direction of war are set within a fluid political context by chief executives in consultation with their principal civil and military advisers. To make sense, Clausewitz's conception of war must be anchored in this concrete political reality. For otherwise, precisely what is the meaning of his celebrated dictum that "war is not only a political act, but a truly political instrument, a continuation of political relations, an implementation of these [relations] by other means, . . . [or rather] by the admixture of other means"? Clausewitz does not see war as a continuation of *diplomacy*—that is, of interstate relations—by other—that is, violent—means. Significantly, he invariably opts for the comprehensive concept of politics, which subsumes diplomacy, thus leaving open the possibility that recourse to war can be not only influenced but, in some instances, even determined by internal political considerations.

Clausewitz himself insists that while "the political *Absicht* is the purpose, war is the means," and that these means cannot be conceived of separately from the ends they are to serve. Granted, he chooses to consider a government's policy as the reflection of an objective national interest to be protected against the equally objective national interests of other states. But Clausewitz posits this national interest as an ideal-typical construct, since he readily concedes that governmental policy "can take a wrong direction as a result of the ambitions, private interests, and pride of the rulers." Once such motives and interests are taken to be normal and standard, rather than "wrong," the political motives and purposes for going to war emerge as being forged in the fire of the political process. Specifically, in the crunch of the decision the principal actors and classes can be expected to calculate whether and how war can serve to establish, maintain, advance, or undermine the political fortunes of influential segmental elites within and outside the government of their own country as well as of target countries.

In an era of mass and revolutionary politics the decision to go to war is very much a political decision. To be sure, even or particularly under tumultuous political conditions decision makers and their advisers—including civil and military experts—feign to stand above or beyond partisanship. They mean to sanctify this nonpartisan posture with spurious incantations about their selfless devotion to an objective national interest which instantly demands the subordination of domestic politics to foreign policy. In reality, however, these decision makers and their advisers continue to be political actors with very tangible social, economic, political, and ideological attachments, if not interests. With rare exceptions these attachments are not dissolved or deactivated by the alleged requirements of the primacy of foreign policy.

It is not without significance that in those situations in which foreign policy actors abide first and foremost by the primacy of domestic politics, they do so furtively rather than openly. Ordinarily, however, these actors, when making foreign policy decisions, including decisions for or against war, are moved—if not consciously, certainly unconsciously—by a mixture of external and internal considerations. With each actor the blend of these two components depends not only on the over-all context of power and politics in which he operates but also on his functional position, his habitual political preferences, and his formal political associations. Even with otherwise relatively apolitical actors, notably permanent officials and experts, the degree of internal political calculation rises under conditions of intense partisan conflict at home and in third countries.

Again it was Clausewitz who noted, quite rightly, that war is more likely to approach its abstract nature of unchained violence when the originating motives are exceptionally ambitious and strong and the prewar tensions singularly acute. Under such taut conditions, once war has started, political purposes recede into the background, and the enemy's unconditional surrender becomes the sole objective. Conversely, the weaker the motives and tensions, the more likely that war will retain its political purposes, to be achieved by timely negotiation.

Here, then, is the paradox. Whereas wars whose motivation and intent are primarily diplomatic and external retain their political purposes, as conceived by Clausewitz, those whose mainsprings are essentially political and internal fail to acquire a well-defined project.

By Clausewitz's criteria wars whose motives and causes are fundamentally—not exclusively—diplomatic and external are and remain essentially political—that is, limited and controlled—in purpose. These are wars that are decided by political actors and classes whose political tenure and social position tend to be secure and who tend to have great latitude for foreign policy decisions. Moreover, though these objectives are likely to precipitate changes in the government and administration of the vanquished power, they neither involve nor require the overthrow of the enemy's regime. In sum, the fabric of legitimacy, both international and national, tends to weather hostilities intact.

As for wars of primarily partisan and internal dynamic, they are decided by political actors and classes whose political tenure and social position tend to be insecure and whose latitude for foreign policy decisions tends to be circumscribed. Precisely because their internal influence and control are tenuous, these actors and classes are inclined to have recourse to external war which, if successful, promises to shore up their faltering position. At the same time rival governments, which probably have internal problems of their own, may consider it opportune to take advantage of this instability. In any case, at the outset even the minimal external objectives of wars that are sparked internally have a tendency to be singularly ill defined. As hostilities unfold these objectives become increasingly indeterminate and ideological and therefore incompatible with the survival of the existing international system. In addition, they are prone to require the overthrow of the regime, rather than of just the government of the defeated power. In sum, the fabric of legitimacy, both international and national, is seriously strained, if not actually torn.[5]

Depending on the intensity and nature of internal instability and conflict, incumbent governments are disposed either against or for foreign-policy pugnacity, including war. Governments tend to refrain from external complications and war if internal disturbances and tensions are so acute that they cannot rely on the loyalty of critical segments not only of the working and peasant population but also of the armed forces. In general terms, "the relation between outer conflict and inner cohesion does not hold true where internal cohesion before the outbreak of the conflict is so low that the group members have ceased to regard preservation of the group as worthwhile, or actually see the outside threat to concern 'them' rather than 'us.' " Under such circumstances "disintegration of the group, rather than increase in cohesion, will be the result of outside conflict."[6] This being the case, unless other powers, vital allies, or reckless internal factions force their hands, governments that face acute internal turmoil or conflict (e.g., strikes, demonstrations, riots) are inclined to avoid a test of arms in which the risks of defeat, and hence of fatal inner convulsions, seem prohibitively high. They may seek to postpone war until shortly after the internal situation has been brought under better control, when mounting external conflict can become part of a political strategy designed to erode the sources for renewed internal unrest. In the meantime, in their bid to recover greater internal control, embattled governments tend to flaunt the specter of external dangers with the calculation that international tensions short of war can help to foster domestic cohesion.[7]

But strained and unstable internal conditions tend to make elites markedly intransigent and disposed to exceptionally drastic, not to say extravagantly hazardous, pre-emptive solutions. Be-

[5] Cf. Richard N. Rosecrance, *Action and Reaction in World Politics* (Boston, 1963), passim.

[6] Lewis Coser, *The Social Functions of Conflict* (New York, 1964), p. 93.

[7] Cf. Jonathan Wilkenfeld, "Domestic and Foreign Conflict Behavior of Nations," *Journal of Peace Research Vol. 5*, no. 1 (1968) pp. 64–65.

leaguered and vulnerable governments and political classes are more likely to be disposed for than against recourse to mounting external conflict or war. By both reflex and calculation they assume that the members of a seriously torn polity and society will pull together once they are confronted with a common and imminent external threat and foe. Such governments incline to use heightened external conflict or war as an instrument of internal cohesion, as an antidote to insurrection, revolution, civil war, or secession that they claim to be imminent. The ultimate objective is to monetize a striking diplomatic or military victory to restore, preferably to enhance, the waning power and prestige of internally enfeebled regimes, governments, and elites.

It appears, then, that the calculus of the internal political effects of intensified external conflict or war is more likely either to deter or to encourage recourse to war in a revolutionary era and under conditions of internal instability than in times of domestic and international equipoise.[8] In troubled times all major leaders, factions, and parties are intensely alive to the internal political uses and abuses of war. They know that the course and outcome of war are bound to have profound political consequences. Whereas victory promises to strengthen those who advocate, direct, and support war, defeat holds in store the opposite fate. At least in the short run, defeat portends a decline in the power and influence of the war party and its institutions, to the advantage of opposition elements. Furthermore, in revolutionary eras political leaders of all persuasions are anxious about the impact of war on the power and prestige of the pacesetting but embattled revolutionary regime, as well as on critical political struggles in third countries.

The view that war has important internal functions has a long lineage. Through the ages writers have glorified the advantages and virtues of war for individual man. In spite of or because of

---

[8] See my schematic case study "Domestic Causes of the First World War," in *The Responsibility of Power,* ed. Leonard Krieger and Fritz Stern (New York, 1967), chap. 15.

all its brutalities, until very recently war was said to promote man's virility, biological selection, selflessness, and nobility. The benefits to woman usually were passed over in silence, except that the female was said to bask in the male's heroic comportment, even or especially when it resulted in his death, disability, or disfiguration. Needless to say, these "individual" wages of war are as difficult to measure and verify as such individual motives for war as personal aggressiveness.

In addition to celebrating these reputed gains for the individual, writers sought to demonstrate the benefits for community, society, government, and nation. At these various levels of social existence the payoff was said to be in the form of improved solidarity, cohesion, stability, and prestige. Walter Bagehot and Ludwig Gumplowicz focused on the functions of war in the formation of communities, states, and nations. Other social theorists—notably Aristotle, Machiavelli, Bodin, Montaigne, Treitschke, and Simmel—were concerned with the uses of war in the preservation and consolidation of existing but internally divided or disintegrating societies and polities. They conceived of war as a safety valve for pent-up internal conflicts and tensions, as a deflection of domestic anatagonisms into foreign hostilities.

Bodin's reference to the expediency of using war for internal purposes is a telling illustration of this position:

. . . the best way of preserving a state, and guaranteeing it against sedition, rebellion, and civil war is to keep the subjects in amity one with another, and to this end, to find an enemy against whom they can make common cause. Examples of this can be found in all commonwealths. The Romans are a specially good illustration. They could find no better antidote to civil war, nor one more certain in its effects, than to oppose an enemy to its citizens. On one occasion, when they were engaged in bitter mutual strife, the enemy found his way into the city and seized the Capitol. The citizens instantly composed their differences, and united to expel the enemy. . . . Without looking further afield, we have an example in this kingdom [i.e., France] when it was in grave peril in 1562. The English set foot in France and seized Havre de Grace, whereupon the civil war was abandoned, and the subjects united to make common cause against the enemy. Perceiving which, the English resolved to leave the French to fight one another, and wait till they were thereby altogether ruined, when they might invade the kingdom without difficulty, or the danger of encountering resistance. . . .

Unrestrained freedom inflates men and encourages them to abandon themselves to every sort of vice. Fear however keeps them mindful of their duty. One can have no doubt that the great Ruler and Governor of the whole world, in creating things so that each balanced by its contrary, permits wars and enmities between men to punish them the one by the other, and keep all in fear, for fear is the sole inducement to virtue. When Samuel addressed the people, he told them plainly, that God had raised up enemies against them to keep them humble, and to try, prove, and punish them. *These considerations serve to show how wrong are those who say that the sole end of war is peace* [italics mine]. . . .[9]

Writing in the sixteenth century, Bodin fused the individual and the collective aspects of the internal benefits of war; and he spoke in terms of the state, the citizen, and his civic duty. By the late nineteenth century Treitschke, aware of both dimensions, related them to class divisions. According to this champion of power in politics, "war, with all its brutality, and sternness, weaves a bond of love between man and man, linking them together to face death, and causing all class distinctions to disappear."[10] More recently American theorists of international politics have postulated that acutely beleaguered power and governing elites tend to resort to heightened external tensions or even to war in order to preserve or buttress their precarious internal position.[11]

Montaigne was one of the first to question the rightness of channeling domestic tensions into foreign wars, even if internal chaos should be the price of continued peace. Though he conceded that a "foreign war is a much milder evil than a civil war," he assumed that "God would not favor so unjust an enterprise as to injure and pick a quarrel with others for our own conveni-

[9] Jean Bodin, *Six Books of the Commonwealth*, abr. and trans. M. J. Tooley (Oxford, 1955), pp. 168–69.

[10] Heinrich von Treitschke, *Power Politics*, abr. and ed. Hans Kohn (New York, 1963), p. 245.

[11] Ernest B. Haas and Allen S. Whiting, *Dynamics of International Relations* (New York, 1956), pp. 62–64; and Rosecrance, pp. 304–5.

ence." Even so, Montaigne grudgingly accepted that societies which face fatal internal schisms expediently have recourse to "bad means for a good purpose."[12]

Centuries later the Marxists, rather than question the reality or legitimacy of diversionary wars, probed into their class determinants. In the Marxist scheme capitalist classes deliberately and cunningly whip up nationalist passions and unchain such wars as part of a rearguard action designed to postpone the inevitable proletarian revolution. In sum, Marxists sought to identify the class ties of the political actors who manipulate the safety valve and to uncover the social, economic, and political mainsprings and purposes of this calculated recourse to war.

There are grave objections to the Marxist thesis that shrewd capitalists or their hired hands bring on wars for selfish class objectives. But notwithstanding these objections, the over-all direction of the Marxist inquiry into the causes and objectives of war is altogether sound. In particular, during Europe's most recent era of revolution and counterrevolution (1870–1956), the internal and external mainsprings of war have been thoroughly intertwined. Whereas the diplomatic side of the causes of this era's wars has been thoroughly explored, the domestic side of these wars continues to be neglected. In seeking to correct this imbalance researchers could usefully hypothesize the primacy of domestic politics in international relations. But in this examination of the internal side of the causes of war they will have to enlarge the focus of sclerotic Marxists who confine themselves to examining the class determinants of foreign policy, including the decision to go to war. Researchers will have to take account of the full range of interrelated political, social, economic, and ideological factors and conflicts that condition the making, conduct, and implementation of foreign policy.

In this most recent era of European turmoil the decision for or against war, whenever it presented itself, necessarily became caught up in the struggle between the forces of order and the forces of change. The more intense a given internal crisis, the

---

[12] Michel de Montaigne, *Essais*, bk. 2, chap. 23 ("Des mauvais moyens employez à bonne fin").

greater the erosion of the compromise-seeking center, to the advantage of the collision-bound forces of revolution and counterrevolution. This erosion was as fatal to internal cohesion as it was to external quietude.

As noted above, internal tensions can become so acute that key political actors within or close to the government will counsel extreme caution, if not perilous appeasement, for fear that the exertions of war will fatally strain or transform government and society. More commonly, however, such internal tensions incline political actors and forces to resort to external tensions and war in efforts to salvage or bolster their domestic position.

Since 1870 political actors who tended to favor resort to war for internal purposes looked for support to social and occupational strata, interest groups, and political formations that were anxious, if not panicky, about their life chances in the crisis-torn, modernizing world about them. The appeals of inflamed jingoism and war found particularly strong resonance among nobles, gentry, artisans, small shopkeepers, low-level civil servants, status-seeking degree holders, bypassed entrepreneurs, ex-officers, small peasant proprietors, and the new middle classes. These were the same crisis strata that provided the social bases for counterrevolutionary movements and politics.

In fact, starting with the Franco-Prussian War the politics of counterrevolution and of diversionary war have repeatedly been closely tied, if not completely interlocked. They were activated by the same conservative political leaders, who, doubtful of their ability to master mounting internal dysfunctions, inclined toward the pre-emptive use of force, either at home or abroad. Significantly, the cadres of the bureaucracy, foreign office, army, police, and church either were drawn from or had strong attachments to one or more segments of the crisis strata. For fear of losing the loyalty of these cadres and institutions that are so vital for the maintenance of law and order—let alone for preventive confrontations—otherwise self-confident and compromise-seeking conservatives became responsive to the pressures of counterrevolutionary leaders who counseled recourse to force and violence.

In addition to disposing of a Trojan horse within the government in the form of strategically placed cadres, these counterrevolutionary leaders had another valuable asset. Unlike traditionalists and conservatives, who were reticent and awkward about the populist politics of this age of mass mobilization and manipulation, counterrevolutionaries thrived and excelled in it. Specifically, they propagated mass appeals attributing society's ills to internal, external, or mixed conspiracies. Such formulas were designed to serve a double purpose: they provided a political orientation for social elements that were in danger of succumbing to the rival revolutionary rhetoric, while at the same time they depicted the root evil as one that could and should be destroyed by instant and drastic recourse to force. In any case, the conspiratorial view of politics was peculiarly attractive to anxiety-ridden crisis strata which, instead of trusting the course of history, were impatient to arrest or reverse it. And it was among these strata that counterrevolutionary leaders sought and organized the mass support which, for a price, they put at the service of conservatives. Whether or not conservatives were prepared to pay the price, which could include either a preemptive coup at home or preventive diversionary war abroad, depended on the prospects for internal stability that the counterrevolutionaries themselves did their best to undermine.

In other words, diversionary war tended to be related to the polarization of politics, which, in turn, was a function of the reality or fear of approaching internal chaos. This being so, it is important to study the nature of this polarization between the forces of order and the forces of change; to examine its impact on the making of foreign policy; to identify the social roots and attachments of political actors who, in this situation, advocated external war for internal purposes; and to probe the social bases and the political tactics of those political factions and interest groups which either supported or pressured these actors.

Conservatives and counterrevolutionaries have two ways of lancing an acute crisis situation. One consists of precipitating diversionary war in the expectation that first the war effort and then victory will solidify the political situation to their advantage. The other takes the form of a coup d'état. Depending on the constellation of power and politics, both national and international, this coup d'état may, at a subsequent stage, require external war for survival.

Since not only war but also a coup are solutions of force, the reliability of the army and police is decisive in both. The counterrevolutionary coup is executed if not with the cooperation at least with the connivance of the forces of law and order, including the military and police forces. This option of a coup from above is not open to revolutionaries, who are forced to stage their assault from below.

The year 1848 taught revolutionaries the extreme difficulty and high cost, not to say the impossibility, of a frontal assault on the state. The Paris Commune of 1871 confirmed the lesson that in the face of modernized military and police forces barricades and street fighting become obsolete. The military advantages are increasingly on the side of governments, which can call on skilled officers and men to use the latest artillery, matériel, transport, and communications to suppress insurrections. Furthermore, because of the state's heightened capability and readiness for counterinsurgency, well-disciplined and equipped revolutionary bands or shock troops lose the hitherto significant advantages of surprise attack. As for primitive rebels, though they retain their nuisance value, they cease to be any kind of a serious threat to law and order.

No wonder, therefore, that Engels repeatedly cautioned revolutionaries against playing with insurrection and against letting themselves be provoked into premature street fighting.[13] He realized—and so did many others who lacked his military sophistication—that more than ever all the advantages, both offensive and defensive, were with the antirevolutionary side. Of course, especially once a revolutionary movement has a disciplined vanguard and mass membership, a government afraid of being engulfed and pressed by counterrevolutionary elements may throw

[13] See Friedrich Engels' introduction of March 6, 1895 to Karl Marx, *The Class Struggles in France, 1848–50* (New York, 1935), pp. 13–14, 17, 21–24, 27–29; and Engels, *The German Revolution* (Chicago, 1967), pp. 227–28.

out the kind of pre-emptive challenge that is impossible to refuse, even if the prospects for success are poor.

Under one set of conditions, however, the revolutionary prospects improve drastically. In the event of a world crisis involving the major European powers in war, certain governments might lose their otherwise impregnable position. In particular war saps the capability for internal repression by regimes and governments that are outclassed, ill-prepared, overextended, or defeated on the battlefields.

Here, then, is another paradox. After 1871, certainly in theory though also in practice, socialists either resolutely opposed war or yielded to it reluctantly and under protest. And yet, given the unparalleled order-enforcing capabilities of states and governments that were spared the exertions of taxing external hostilities, it looked increasingly as if only the strains of war could burst the antirevolutionary dam in one country or another.

At the same time, while the radical Left found itself steadily more dependent, in spite of itself, on defeat in war to blaze a revolutionary trail, the Right renewed its trust in military victory to buttress its failing political fortunes. But, unlike the Left, the Right kept the option of using the military and police cudgels to break its enemies at home before seeking the destruction of enemies abroad.

When the examination of the causes and objectives of war centers on decision making in one of the belligerent countries, the analytic and explicative weight falls on its domestic and political rather than on its external and diplomatic life. But since it takes at least two sovereign states to make war, and since the decisions of as yet uncommitted governments can decisively influence the course of events, this focus needs to be enlarged. It must be expanded to encompass decision making not only in nations set on a collision course but also in third nations whose stand is likely to affect the balance of international power. Needless to say, it is important to take account of the nature of the regimes and the political systems within which political actors face and manipulate this interplay of internal and external conflict. The necessity, possibility, and scope for manipulation may differ according to whether authority systems are autocratic or democratic.[14]

In other words, even though the diplomatic and military points at which two or more nations touch constitute the critical nexus, the causes and objectives of war cannot be deduced from the minutes of bilateral or multilateral negotiations or the texts of foreign office dispatches. These reflect immediate bargaining considerations and only rarely, if ever, political concerns which guide, possibly determine, diplomatic negotiations. Granted, the choice of specific diplomatic issues or objectives is not necessarily influenced to any significant degree by political or partisan calculations. However, the flexibility with which negotiators or envoys approach diplomatic issues cannot be divorced from their own and their opposites' internal political coordinates.

In the perspective of pure diplomacy—cabinet diplomacy in an era that is essentially stable, both internationally and domestically —it may well be possible to prescribe a correct policy for the statesmen of nations that have been singled out as targets for diversionary war. But if the governments of the target nations are under acute internal pressures themselves, this "correct" policy may be difficult if not impossible to follow. The governments of all the participating and affected nations find themselves guided by considerations of domestic politics rather than by calculations of raison d'état.

But in addition to taking account of the political needs of their own governments, diplomatic actors seek to influence the internal situation in other nations to their own advantage. This requires not only that they be accurately informed about internal developments there but also that they have the political astuteness to use that intelligence wisely and effectively. Depending on the circumstances, the indicated diplomatic course may be one of provocation, obduracy, appeasement, or temporization.

Under conditions of mass politics this double-edged politicization of diplomacy is intimately related to or grafted upon the

---

[14] Wilkenfeld, esp. pp. 57, 60, 63–67.

equally politicized making of foreign policy. In times of instability, both internal and external, this all pervasive politicization is proof that international relations, including war, have become an extension and a tool of domestic politics.

Selected Bibliography

Bias in the Social Sciences

✓ Bretton, Hugh. *The Political Sciences: General Principles of Selection in Social Science and History.* New York: Basic Books, 1970.

Bukharin, Nikolai. *Historical Materialism: A System of Sociology.* New York: International Publishers, 1928.

Gouldner, Alvin. *The Coming Crisis of Western Sociology.* New York: Basic Books, 1970.

Lukacs, Georg. *Geschichte und Klassenbewustsein.* Neuwied and Berlin: Luchterhand, 1962.

✓ Myrdal, Gunnar. *Objectivity in Social Research.* New York: Pantheon, 1969.

Piaget, Jean. *Le Structuralisme.* Paris: Presses Universitaires, 1968.

Zeitlin, Irving. *Ideology and the Development of Sociological Theory.* Englewood Cliffs, N.J.: Prentice-Hall, 1968.

Theoretical Guideposts

*‡ Adorno, T. W., Frenkel-Brunswik, Else, et al. *The Authoritarian Personality.* New York: Harper & Brothers, 1950.

Amann, Peter H. "Revolution: A Redefinition." *Political Science Quarterly,* vol. 77, no. 1 (March 1962), pp. 36–53.

*‡ Arendt, Hannah. *The Origins of Totalitarianism,* 3d ed. New York: Harcourt Brace, 1966.

Baechler, Jean. *Les Phénomènes révolutionnaires.* Paris: Presses Universitaires, 1970.

Bettelheim, Bruno, and Janowitz, Morris. *Dynamics of Prejudice: A Psychological and Sociological Study of Veterans.* New York: Harper & Brothers, 1950.

‡ Black, C. E. *The Dynamics of Modernization: A Study in Comparative History.* New York: Harper & Row, 1966.

---

* Important for historical insight, conceptual formulation, and/or exemplary method.

† For further bibliographic leads.

‡ Available in paperback.

Bodin, Louis. *Les Intellectuels,* 2d ed. Paris: Presses Universitaires, 1964.

* Bois, Paul. *Paysans de l'Ouest.* Le Mans: Vilaire, 1960.

Brinkman, Carl. *Soziologische Theorie der Revolution.* Göttingen: Vandenhoeck and Ruprecht, 1948.

*‡ Brinton, Crane. *The Anatomy of Revolution,* rev. ed. Englewood Cliffs, N.J.: Prentice Hall, 1952.

Burrowes, Robert. "Totalitarianism: The Revised Standard Version." *World Politics,* vol. XXI, no. 2 (January 1969), pp. 272–94.

Camus, Albert. *L'Homme révolté.* Paris: Gallimard, 1951.

Chorley, Katherine C. *Armies and the Art of Revolution.* London: Faber and Faber, 1943.

* Christie, R., and Jehoda, M., eds. *Studies in the Scope and Methods of the Authoritarian Personality.* Glencoe, Ill.: Free Press, 1954.

‡ Cohn, Norman. *The Pursuit of the Millennium: Revolutionary Messianism in Medieval and Reformation Europe and Its Bearing on Modern Totalitarian Movements.* New York: Oxford, 1957.

‡ Debray, Régis. *Revolution in the Revolution?* New York: Monthly Review Press, 1967.

Decouflé, André. *Sociologie des Révolutions.* Paris: Presses Universitaires, 1968.

Dimier, L. *Les Maîtres de la contre-révolution au dix-neuvième siècle.* Paris: Librairie des Saints-Pères, 1907.

Eckstein, Harry, ed. *Internal War: Problems and Approaches.* New York: Free Press-Macmillan, 1964.

Edwards, Lyford P. *The Natural History of Revolution.* Chicago: University of Chicago Press, 1927.

‡ Engels, Friedrich. *The German Revolutions: The Peasant War in Germany* and *Germany: Revolution and Counterrevolution.* Chicago: University of Chicago Press, 1967.

* Escarpit, Robert. *Sociologie de la Littérature,* 4th ed. Paris: Presses Universitaires, 1968.

Fraenkel, Ernst. *Zur Soziologie der Klassenjustiz.* Berlin: Laubsche, 1927.

‡ Friedrich, Carl J., ed. *Totalitarianism.* Cambridge, Mass.: Harvard University Press, 1954.

*‡ Friedrich, Carl J., and Brzezinski, Zbigniew K. *Totalitarian Dictatorship and Autocracy,* 1st and 2d ed. Cambridge, Mass.: Harvard University Press, 1956 and 1965.

* Geiger, Theodor. *Die Masse und ihre Aktion: Ein Beitrag zur Soziologie der Revolution.* Stuttgart: Enke, 1926.

* Germani, G. "Fascism and Class." In ‡ S. J. Woolf, ed., *The Nature of Fascism* (New York: Random House, 1968), pp. 65–95.

‡ Gerth, H. H., and Mills, C. Wright. *From Max Weber: Essays in Sociology*. New York: Oxford, 1946.

Griewank, Karl. *Der neuzeitliche Revolutionsbegriff*. Weimar: Böhlaus, 1955.

* Groth, Alexander J. "The 'Isms' in Totalitarianism." *American Political Science Review*, vol. LVIII, no. 4 (December 1964), pp. 888–901.

‡ Hallgarten, George W. F. *Why Dictators?: The Causes and Forms of Tyrannical Rule Since 600 B.C.* New York: Macmillan, 1954.

Heer, Friedrich. "Der Konservative und die Reaktion." *Die Neue Rundschau*, vol. 69, no. 1 (1958), pp. 490–527.

Huntington, Samuel P. "Conservatism as an Ideology." *American Political Science Review*, vol. LI, no. 2 (June 1957), pp. 454–73.

*‡ Johnson, Chalmers. *Revolution and the Social System*. Hoover Institution Studies: 3, Stanford University, 1964.

‡ Johnson, Chalmers. *Revolutionary Change*. Boston: Little, Brown, 1966.

Kann, Robert A. *The Problem of Restoration: A Study in Comparative Political History*. Berkeley: University of California Press, 1968.

*‡ Kecskemeti, Paul. *Strategic Surrender: The Politics of Victory and Defeat*. Stanford: Stanford University Press, 1958.

*‡ Kirchheimer, Otto. *Political Justice: The Use of Legal Procedures for Political Ends*. Princeton: Princeton University Press, 1961.

* Kirchheimer, Otto. "Confining Conditions and Revolutionary Breakthroughs." *The American Political Science Review*, vol. 59, no. 4 (December 1963), pp. 964–74.

‡ Kirk, Russell. *The Conservative Mind*, 3d rev. ed. Chicago: Regnery, 1960.

* Kolnai, Aurel. "Gegenrevolution." *Kölner Vierteljahrshefte für Soziologie*, vol. X, nos. 1–2 (1931–1932), pp. 171–99, 295–319.

*† Kornhauser, William. *The Politics of Mass Society*. Glencoe, Ill.: Free Press, 1959.

Koselleck, R. "Der neuzeitliche Revolutionsbegriff als geschichtliche Kategorie." *Studium Generale*, vol. 22, fasc. 8 (August 8, 1969), pp. 824–40.

Labrousse, Ernest. "1848–1830–1789: Comment naissent les révolutions." *Actes du Congrès historique du centenaire de la révolution de 1848* (Paris: Presses Universitaires, 1948), pp. 1–29.

‡ Lasswell, Harold D. *Psychopathology and Politics*, new ed. New York: The Viking Press, 1960.

* Lasswell, Harold D., and Lerner, Daniel, eds. *World Revolutionary Elites: Studies in Coercive Ideological Movements.* Cambridge, Mass.: M.I.T. Press, 1965.

‡ Leiden, Carl, and Schmitt, Karl M., eds. *The Politics of Violence: Revolution in the Modern World.* Englewood Cliffs, N.J.: Prentice-Hall, 1968.

Lederer, Emil. *State of the Masses.* New York: Norton, 1940.

Lenin, V. I. *Collected Works,* vol. XXI, bk. II. New York: International Publishers, 1932, pp. 147–247 (*State and Revolution*).

‡ Lipset, Seymour Martin. *Political Man: The Social Bases of Politics.* Garden City, N.Y.: Doubleday, 1960. Chapter 5.

Lipset, Seymour Martin, and Rabb, Earl. *The Politics of Unreason: Right-Wing Extremism in America, 1790–1970.* New York: Harper & Row, 1970. Chapters 1, 11–12.

* Lukacs, Georg. *Die Zerstörung der Vernunft.* Neuwied and Berlin: Luchterhand, 1962.

Luttwak, Edward. *Coup d'Etat.* New York: Knopf, 1969.

* McClosky, Herbert. "Conservatism and Personality." *American Political Science Review,* vol. LII, no. 1 (March 1958), pp. 27–45.

Malaparte, Curzio. *Coup d'Etat: The Technique of Revolution.* New York: E. P. Dutton, 1932.

* Mannheim, Karl. *Essays on Sociology and Social Psychology.* New York: Oxford, 1953. Especially chapter 2.

✓* Mannheim, Karl. *Essays on the Sociology of Knowledge.* New York: Oxford, 1952.

Marx, Karl. *The Civil War in France.* New York: International Publishers, 1940.

———. *Class Struggles in France, 1848–1850.* New York: International Publishers, 1935.

✓ ———. *The Eighteenth of Brumaire of Louis Bonaparte.* New York: International Publishers, [?].

———. *Politische Schriften,* ed. Hans-Joachim Lieber, 2 vols. Stuttgart: Cotta-Verlag, 1960–1962.

Marx-Engels-Lenin-Stalin. *Zur deutschen Geschichte,* vol. II. Berlin: Dietz, 1954.

Meisel, James H. *Counterrevolution: How Revolutions Die.* New York: Atherton Press, 1966.

✓ *‡ Michels, Robert. *Political Parties.* Glencoe, Ill.: The Free Press, 1949. Especially chapters 1 and 2.

* Monnerot, Jules. *Sociologie de la Révolution.* Paris: Fayard, 1969.

* Mornet, Daniel. *Les Origines intellectuelles de la révolution française*, 6th ed. Paris: Colin, 1967.

Muhlenfeld, Hans. *Politik ohne Wunschbilder: Die konservative Aufgabe unserer Zeit*. Munich: Oldenbourg, 1952.

* Neumann, Franz L. "Anxiety and Politics." In ‡ Herbert Marcuse, ed., *The Democratic and the Authoritarian State* (Glencoe, Ill.: Free Press, 1957), chapter 11.

* Neumann, Franz L. "Notes on the Theory of Dictatorship." In ‡ Marcuse, ed., *The Democratic and the Authoritarian State*, chapter 9.

*‡ Ostrogorski, Moisei. *Democracy and the Organization of Political Parties*, 2 vols. London: Macmillan, 1902.

* Parsons, Talcott. "Some Sociological Aspects of the Fascist Movements." In Parsons, *Essays in Sociological Theory*, rev. ed. (Glencoe, Ill.: Free Press, 1954), pp. 124–41.

Pettee, George S. *The Process of Revolution*. New York: Harper & Brothers, 1938.

Proudhon, P.-J. *General Idea of the Revolution in the Nineteenth Century*. London: Freedom Press, 1923.

*‡ Rogin, Michael Paul. *The Intellectuals and McCarthy: The Radical Specter*. Cambridge, Mass.: M.I.T. Press, 1967.

Rosenstock-Huessy, Eugen. *Die europäischen Revolutionen*. Jena: Diederichs, 1931.

Rubel, Maximilien. *Karl Marx devant le bonapartisme*. Paris: Mouton, 1960.

* Sartre, Jean-Paul. *Situations*, 6 vols. Paris: Gallimard, 1947–1964.

* Schieder, Theodor. "Das Problem der Revolution im 19. Jahrhundert." *Historische Zeitschrift*, vol. 170, no. 2 (September 1950), pp. 233–71.

*‡ Seton-Watson, Hugh. *Neither War nor Peace: The Struggle for Power in the Postwar World*. New York: Praeger, 1960. Especially chapter 7, "The Seizure of Power."

* Sherif, Muzafer. *In Common Predicament: Social Psychology of Intergroup Conflict and Cooperation*. Boston: Houghton Mifflin, 1966.

Snow, Vernon. "The Concept of Revolution in Seventeenth-Century England." *The Historical Journal*, vol. V, no. 2 (1962), pp. 167–74.

‡ Sorel, Georges. *Reflections on Violence*. New York: The Free Press, 1950.

Sorokin, Pitrim A. *The Sociology of Revolution*. Philadelphia: Lippincott, 1925.

*‡ Syme, Ronald. *The Roman Revolution*. Oxford: Clarendon, 1939.

°‡ Tilly, Charles. *The Vendée*. Cambridge, Mass.: Harvard University Press, 1964.

Tucker, Robert C. "The Dictator and Totalitarianism." *World Politics*, vol. XVII, no. 4 (July 1965), pp. 555–83.

‡ Vagts, Alfred. *A History of Militarism*, rev. ed. Cleveland: Meridian Books, 1959.

° Vidalenc, Jean. *Les Emigrés français, 1789–1825*. Caen, 1963.

° Walter, Eugene Victor. *Terror and Resistance: A Study of Political Violence*. New York: Oxford, 1969.

Wormser-Migot, Olga. *L'Ere Concentrationnaire*. Paris: Culture, Arts, Loisirs, 1970.

Prewar Europe

GENERAL

°‡ Barraclough, Goeffrey. *An Introduction to Contemporary History*. New York: Basic Books, 1964.

†‡ Gilbert, Felix. *The End of the European Era: 1890 to the Present*. New York: Norton, 1970.

°‡ Hayes, Carlton, J. H. *A Generation of Materialism, 1871–1900*. New York: Harper, 1941.

Hughes, H. Stuart. *Contemporary Europe*, 2d ed. Englewood Cliffs, N.J.: Prentice-Hall, 1966.

‡ Masur, Gerhard. *Prophets of Yesterday: Studies in European Culture, 189–1914*. New York: Macmillan, 1961.

‡ Roberts, J. M. *Europe, 1880–1945*. New York: Holt, Rinehart and Winston, 1967.

Watt, D. C., Spencer, Frank, and Brown, Neville. *A History of the World in the Twentieth Century*. Chicago: Scott, Foresman, 1968.

THE COMMUNE

Annales de l'Assemblée Nationale. *Enquête sur l'Insurrection du 18 mars 1871*, 3 vols. Paris, 1872.

Brabant, Frank H. *The Beginning of the Third Republic: A History of the National Assembly, February–September 1871*. London: Macmillan, 1940.

Bourgin, Georges, ed. *La Guerre de 1870–71 et la Commune*. Paris: Editions Nationales, 1939.

Bruhat, J., Dautry, J., and Tersen, E. *La Commune de 1871*. Paris: Editions Ouvrières, 1960.

Claretie, Jules. *Histoire de le Révolution de 1870–71*, 2 vols. Paris: Aux Bureaux du Journal *l'Eclipse*, 1872.

Du Camp, Maxine. *Les Convulsions de Paris*, 5th ed. Paris: Hachette, 1881.

Horne, Alistaire. *The Fall of Paris: The Siege and the Commune 1870– 71*. New York: St. Martin's Press, 1965.

†‡ Jellinek, Frank. *The Paris Commune of 1871*. New York: Grosset and Dunlap, 1965.

Lidsky, Paul. *Les Ecrivains contre la Commune*. Paris: Maspero, 1970.

* Lissagaray, P.-O. *Histoire de la Commune de 1871*, new ed. Paris: E. Dentus, 1896.

* Rougerie, Jacques. *Procès des Communards*. Paris: Julliard, 1964.

Schnerb, Robert. *Rouher et le Second Empire*. Paris: Colin, 1949.

THE NEW IMPERIALISM

Battaglia, Roberto. *La prima guerra d'Africa*. Turin: Einaudi, 1958.

* Brunschwig, Henri. *Mythes et Réalités de l'impérialisme colonial français, 1871–1914*. Paris: Colin, 1960.

Ganiage, Jean. *Les Origines du protectorat français en Tunisie, 1861– 1881*. Paris: Presses Universitaires, 1959.

Gollwitzer, Heinz. *Europe in the Age of Imperialism, 1880–1914*. New York: Harcourt, Brace and World, 1969.

Malozemoff, Andrew. *Russian Far Eastern Policy, 1881–1904*. Berkeley: University of California Press, 1958.

Miège, Jean-Louis. *L'Impérialisme colonial italien de 1870 à nos jours*. Paris: Societé d'Edition d'enseignement supérieur, 1968.

* Platt, D. C. M. "Economic Factors in British Policy During the 'New Imperialism'." *Past and Present*, no. 39 (April 1968), pp. 120–38.

Pogge von Strandmann, Hartmut. "Domestic Origins of Germany's Colonial Expansion under Bismarck." *Past and Present*, no. 42 (February 1969), pp. 140–59.

Porter, Bernard. *Critics of Empire*. New York: St. Martin's Press, 1969.

‡ Robinson, Roland, and Gallagher, John. *Africa and the Victorians: The Official Mind of Imperialism*. London: Macmillan, 1961.

*‡ Semmel, Bernard. *Imperialism and Social Reform: English Social-Imperial Thought, 1895–1914*. London: George Allen and Unwin, 1960.

Sieberg, Howard. *Eugène Etienne und die französische Kolonialpolitik, 1887–1904*. Opland: Westdeutscher Verlag, 1968.

‡ Thornton, A. P. *The Imperial Idea and Its Enemies: A Study in British Power.* London: Macmillan, 1959.

Wehler, Hans-Ulrich. *Bismarck und der Imperialismus.* Cologne: Kiepenheuer and Witsch, 1969.

ENGLAND

Blake, Robert. *The Unknown Prime Minister: The Life and Times of Andrew Bonar Law, 1858–1923.* London: Eyre and Spottiswoode, 1955.

Callwell, C. E., ed. *Field Marshall Sir Henry Wilson: His Life and Diaries,* 2 vols. London: Cassell, 1927.

Colvin, Ian. *The Life of Carson,* 3 vols. London: Victor Gollancz, 1932–36.

Cross, Colin. *The Liberals in Power, 1905–1914.* London: Barrie and Rockliff, 1963.

*‡ Dangerfield, George. *The Strange Death of Liberal England, 1910–1914.* New York: Smith, 1935.

Fergusson, Sir James. *The Curragh Incident.* London: Faber and Faber, 1964.

Gollin, A. M. *The Observer and J. L. Garvin, 1908–1914.* London: Oxford, 1960.

Gollin, A. M. *Proconsul in Politics: A Study of Lord Milner in Opposition and in Power.* London: Anthony Blond, 1964.

* Guttsman, W. L. *The British Political Elite.* New York: Basic Books, 1963.

*‡ Halévy, Élie. *The Rule of Democracy, 1905–1914.* London: Ernest Benn, 1934.

Hearnshaw, F. J. C. *Conservatism in England: An Analytical, Historical, and Political Survey.* London: Macmillan, 1933.

Hyde, H. Montgomery. *Carson.* London: Heinemann, 1953.

Jones, J. R. "England." In Hans Rogger and Eugen Weber, eds., *The European Right* (Berkeley: University of California Press, 1965), pp. 29–70.

Marcus, Geoffrey. *Before the Lamps Went Out.* London: George Allen and Unwin, 1965.

Nowell-Smith, Simon, ed. *Edwardian England, 1901–1914.* London: Oxford, 1964.

Scally, Robert J. *The Sources of the National Coalition of 1916: A Political History of British Social Imperialism.* Unpublished Ph.D. thesis, Princeton University, 1967.

Stewart, A. T. Q. *The Ulster Crisis.* London: Faber and Faber, 1967.

Strauss, E. *Irish Nationalism and British Democracy*. London: Methuen, 1951.

Thompson, F. M. L. *English Landed Society in the Nineteenth Century*. London: Routledge and Kegan Paul, 1963.

FRANCE

Buthman, William Curt. *The Rise of Integral Nationalism in France*. New York: Columbia University Press, 1939.

Cairns, John C. "Politics and Foreign Policy: The French Parliament, 1911–1914." *The Canadian Historical Review*, vol. XXXIV, no. 3 (September 1953), pp. 245–76.

Calhoun, Fryar. *Politics of Internal Order: French Government and Labor Opposition, 1898–1914*. Unpublished Ph. D. thesis, Princeton University, 1971.

Chapman, Geoffrey W. *The Political Mainsprings of International Conflict: France, Italy and the First World War*. Unpublished Ph. D. thesis, Princeton University, Part One.

Clauss, Max. *Das politische Frankreich vor dem Kriege*. Karlsruhe: G. Braun, 1928.

Frank, Walter. *Nationalismus und Demokratie im Frankreich der dritten Republik, 1871–1918*. Hamburg: Hanseatische Verlagsanstalt, 1933.

Michon, Georges. *L'Alliance Franco-Russe, 1891–1917*. Paris: A. Delpeuch, 1927.

———. *La Préparation à la guerre: La loi des trois ans, 1910–1914*. Paris: Rivière, 1935.

° Shapiro, David, ed. *The Right in France, 1890–1919*. London: Chatto and Windus, 1962.

° Sumler, David E. *Polarization in French Politics, 1909–1914*. Unpublished Ph.D. thesis, Princeton University, 1968.

Weber, Eugen. *The Nationalist Revival in France, 1905–1914*. Berkeley: University of California Press, 1959.

ITALY

Chapman, Geoffrey W. *The Political Mainsprings of International Conflict: France, Italy and the First World War*. Unpublished Ph. D. thesis, Princeton University, 1971. Part Two.

† Renzi, William A. "Italy's Neutrality and Entrance into the Great War: A Reexamination." *American Historical Review*, vol. LXXIII, no. 5 (June 1968), pp. 1414–32.

Rosen, E. R. "Italiens Kriegseintritt im Jahre 1915 als innenpolitisches Problem der Giolitti Aera." *Historische Zeitschrift,* vol. 187, no. 2 (April 1959), pp. 289–363.

Salomone, A. William. *Italy in the Giolittian Era: Italian Democracy in the Making, 1900–1914,* new ed. Philadelphia: University of Pennsylvania Press, 1960.

Thayer, John A. *Italy and the Great War: Politics and Culture, 1870–1915.* Madison and Milwaukee: University of Wisconsin Press, 1964.

Vigezzi, Brunello. *Da Giolitti a Salandra.* Florence: Vallecchi, 1969.

—— *L'Italia di fronte alla prima guerra mondiale.* Milan: Ricciardi, 1966.

* Webster, Richard A. "From Insurrection to Intervention: The Italian Crisis of 1914." *Italian Quarterly,* vols. 5–6, nos. 20–21 (Winter 1961/Spring 1962), pp. 27–50.

GERMANY

* Anderson, Pauline R. *The Background of Anti-English Feeling in Germany, 1890–1902.* Washington, D.C.: American University Press, 1939.

Fischer, Fritz. *Krieg der Illusionen: Die deutsche Politik von 1911 bis 1914.* Düsseldorf: Droste, 1969.

Frank, Walter. *Hofprediger Adolf Stoecker und die christlichsoziale Bewegung,* 2d ed. Hamburg: Hanseatische Verlagsanstalt, 1935.

Kaelble, Hartmut. *Industrielle Interessenpolitik in der wilhelminischen Gesellschaft: Centralverband Deutscher Industrieller, 1895–1914.* Berlin: De Gruyter, 1967.

* Kehr, Eckart. *Der Primat der Innenpolitik.* Berlin: De Gruyter, 1965.

——. *Schlachtflottenbau und Parteipolitik: Versuch eines Querschnitts durch die innenpolitischen, sozialen und ideologischen Voraussetzungen des deutschen Imperialismus.* Berlin: Ebering, 1930.

Kitchen, Martin. *The German Officer Corps, 1890–1914.* Oxford: Clarendon, 1968.

* Massing, Paul W. *Rehearsal for Destruction: A Study of Political Anti-Semitism in Imperial Germany.* New York: Harper, 1949.

Nipperdey, Thomas. *Die Organisation der deutschen Parteien vor 1918.* Düsseldorf: Droste, 1961.

Pogge von Strandmann, Hartmut. "Staatsstreichpläne, Alldeutsche und Bethmann Hollweg." In *Hamburger Studien zur neueren Geschichte,* vol. 2 (Frankfurt: Europäische Verlagsanstalt, 1965), pp. 7–45.

* Puhle, Hans-Jürgen. *Agrarische Interessenpolitik und preussicher Konservatismus im wilhelminischen Reich, 1893–1914.* Hanover: Verlag für Literatur und Zeitgeschehen, 1967.

‡ Pulzer, P. G. J. *The Rise of Political Anti-Semitism in Germany and Austria.* New York: John Wiley, 1964.

Röhl, J. C. G. *Germany Without Bismarck: The Crisis of Government in the Second Reich, 1890–1900.* London: Batsford, 1967.

† Sheean, James J. "Germany, 1890–1918: A Survey of Recent Research." *Central European History,* vol. I, no. 4 (December 1968), pp. 345–72.

* Stenkewitz, K. *Gegen Bajonett und Dividende: Die politische Krise in Deutschland am Vorabend des ersten Weltkrieges.* Berlin: Rütten and Loening, 1960.

‡ Stern, Fritz. *The Politics of Cultural Despair: A Study in the Rise of the Germanic Ideology.* Berkeley: University of California Press, 1961.

Wertheimer, Mildred. *The Pan-German League, 1890–1914.* New York: Columbia University Press, 1924.

Zechlin, Egmont. *Staatsstreichpläne Bismarcks und Wilhelm II, 1890–1894.* Stuttgart and Berlin: Cotta, 1929.

AUSTRO-HUNGARIAN EMPIRE

Dedijer, Vladimir. *The Road to Sarajevo.* New York: Simon and Schuster, 1966.

‡ Jászi, Oscar. *The Dissolution of the Hapsburg Monarchy.* Chicago: University of Chicago Press, 1929.

Macartney, C. A. *The Hapsburg Empire, 1790–1981.* London: Weidenfeld and Nicolson, 1968.

May, Arthur J. *The Hapsburg Monarchy, 1867–1914.* Cambridge, Mass.: Harvard University Press, 1960.

* Schorske, Carl E. "Politics in a New Key: An Austrian Triptych." *Journal of Modern History,* vol. XXXIX, no. 4 (December 1967), pp. 343–86.

Skalnik, Kurt. *Dr. Karl Lueger.* Vienna: Herold, 1954.

Stone, Norman. "Hungary and the Crisis of July 1914." *Journal of Contemporary History,* vol. I, no. 3 (1966), pp. 153–70.

Warren, J. C. P. *The Political Career and Influence of Georg Ritter von Schoenerer.* Unpublished Ph.D. thesis, University of London, 1963.

Whiteside, Andrew G. *Austrian National Socialism Before 1918.* The Hague: Mouton, 1962.

RUSSIA

Bernstein, L. *Les Cent noires ou les nationalistes russes*. Paris, 1907.
Bestuzhev, I. V. "Russian Foreign Policy, February-June 1914." *Journal of Contemporary History*, vol. I, no. 3 (1966), pp. 93–112.
‡ Charques, Richard. *The Twilight of Imperial Russia*. London: Oxford University Press, 1958.
*‡ Cherniavsky, Michael, ed. *Prologue to Revolution: Notes of A. N. Iakhontov on the Secret Meetings of the Council of Ministers, 1915*. Englewood Cliffs, N.J.: Prentice-Hall, 1967.
Chernovskii, A., ed. *Soiuz russkogo naroda*. Moscow/Leningrad: Gosudarstvennoe izdatel'stvo, 1929.
Chmielewski, Edward. "Stolypin's Last Crisis." *California Slavic Studies*, vol. III (1964), pp. 95–126.
‡ Cohn, Norman. *Warrant for Genocide*. London: Eyre and Spottiswoode, 1967.
Curtiss, John Sheldon. *Church and State in Russia: The Last Years of the Empire, 1900–1917*. New York: Columbia University Press, 1940.
Jablonowski, Horst. "Die russischen Rechtsparteien, 1905–1917." In *Schriftenreihe Osteuropa: Russland Studien*, No. 3 (Stuttgart, 1957), pp. 43–55.
Jablonowski, Horst. "Die Stellungnahme der russischen Parteien zur Aussenpolitik der Regierung von der russisch-englischen Verständigung bis zum ersten Weltkrieg." In *Forschungen zur Osteuropäischen Geschichte*, vol. V (Berlin, 1957), pp. 60–92.
Die Judenpogrome in Russland. Herausgegeben im Auftrage des Zionistischen Hilfsfonds in London von der zur Erforschung der Pogrome eingesetzten Kommission, 2 vols. Cologne/Leipzig: Jüdischer Verlag, 1910.
Kochan, Lionel. *Russia in Revolution, 1890–1918*. London: Weidenfeld and Nicolson, 1966.
Kovalevsky, Maxime. "La Contre-Révolution en Russie." *Revue de Politique Internationale*, vol. II (Paris, 1914), pp. 1–22, 156–84.
Kropotkin, P. A. *The Terror in Russia*. London: Methuen, 1909.
Kucherov, Samuel. *Courts, Lawyers, and Trials Under the Last Three Tsars*. New York: Praeger, 1953.
* Levin, Alfred. *The Reactionary Tradition in the Election Campaign to the Third Duma*. Oklahoma State University Publication, vol. 59 (1962).
*‡Robinson, Geroid T. *Rural Russia under the Old Regime*. New York: Macmillan, 1932.

Rogger, Hans. "The Beilis Case: Anti-Semitism and Politics in the Reign of Nicholas I." *American Slavic and East European Review,* vol. XXV, no. 4 (December 1964), pp. 615–29.

――. "The Formation of the Russian Right, 1900–1906." *California Slavic Studies,* vol. III (1964), pp. 66–94.

――. "Russia in 1914." *Journal of Contemporary History,* vol. I, no. 4 (1966), pp. 95–119.

* ――. "Was There a Russian Fascism?" *Journal of Modern History,* vol. XXXVI, no. 4 (December 1964), pp. 398–415.

‡ Seton-Watson, Hugh. *The Decline of Imperial Russia, 1855–1914.* New York: Praeger, 1956.

Walsh, W. B. "Political Parties in the Russian Dumas." *Journal of Modern History,* vol. XXII, no. 2 (June 1950), pp. 144–50.

Europe, 1917–1945

REPRESSION, 1918–1920

Badia, Gilbert. *Le Spartakisme.* Paris: L'Arche, 1967.

Beyer, Hans. *Von der Novemberrevolution zur Räterepublik in München.* Berlin: Rütten and Loening, 1957.

Binkley, George A. *The Volunteer Army and Allied Intervention in South Russia, 1917–1921: A Study in the Politics and Diplomacy of the Russian Civil War.* Notre Dame, Ind.: University of Notre Dame Press, 1966.

† Bosl, Karl, ed. *Bayern im Umbruch: Die Revolution von 1918.* Munich and Vienna: Oldenbourg, 1969.

Gratz, Gusztàv. *A forradalmak kora: Magyarország története, 1918–1920.* Budapest, 1935.

Jászi, Oskar. *Magyariens Schuld, Ungarns Sühne: Revolution und Gegenrevolution in Ungarn.* Munich: Verlag für Kulturpolitik, 1923.

Mitchell, Allen. *Revolution in Bavaria, 1918–1919: The Eisner Regime and the Soviet Republic.* Princeton: Princeton University Press, 1965.

Nagy, Zsuzsa L. *Forradalom és ellenforradalom a Dunántúlon.* Budapest, 1961.

Naida, S. F., et al., eds. *Istoriia grazhdanskoi voiny v SSSR, 1917–1922,* 3 vols. Moscow: Gospolitizdat, 1959.

Nemes, Dezso. *Az ellenforradalom története Magyarországon, 1919–1921.* Budapest, 1962.

Pogány, Joseph. *Der weisse Terror in Ungarn.* Vienna, 1920.

Pokrovskii, M. N. *Kontr-revoliutsiia za 4 goda.* Moscow: Gosizdat, 1922.

Pròn, Pàl. *A határban a halál kaszál: Fejezetek-feljegyzéseiböl.* Budapest, 1963.

Stewart, George. *The White Armies of Russia: A Chronicle of Counter-Revolution and Allied Intervention.* New York: Macmillan, 1933.

Subbotovsky, I., ed. *Soiuzniki, russkie reaktsionery i interventsiia: kratkii obzor.* Leningrad: Gosizdat, 1926.

Tarcali, Robert. *Quand Horthy est roi.* Paris: Astra, 1922.

Varjassy, Louis. *Révolution, Bolschevisme, Réaction.* Paris: Jouve, 1934.

‡ Waite, Robert G. L. *Vanguard of Nazism: The Free Corps Movement in Postwar Germany, 1918–1923.* Cambridge, Mass.: Harvard University Press, 1952.

Waldman, Eric. *The Spartacist Uprising of 1919.* Milwaukee: Marquette University Press, 1958.

FASCISM: GENERAL WORKS

‡ Carsten, Francis L. *The Rise of Fascism.* London: Batsford, 1967.

Journal of Contemporary History, vol. 1, no. 1 (1966): International Fascism, 1920–1945.

†‡ Nolte, Ernst. *Die faschistischen Bewegungen: Die Krise des liberalen Systems und die Entwicklung der Faschismen.* Munich: Deutscher Taschenbuch Verlag, 1966.

†‡ Rogger, Hans, and Weber, Eugen, ed. *The European Right: A Historical Profile.* Berkeley: University of California Press, 1965.

Sforza, Count Carlo. *Dictateurs et Dictatures de l'après-guerre.* Paris: Gallimard, 1931.

‡ Weber, Eugen, ed. *Varieties of Fascism.* Princeton, N. J.: Van Nostrand, 1964.

†‡ Woolf, S. J., ed. *European Fascism.* New York: Random House, 1968.

FASCISM: INTERPRETATIONS

* Abendroth, Wolfgang, ed. *Faschismus und Kapitalismus: Theorien über die sozialen Ursprünge und die Funktion des Faschismus.* Frankfurt: Europäische Verlagsanstalt, 1967.

Bardèche, Maurice. *Qu'est-ce que le Fascisme?* Paris: Les Sept Couleurs, 1961.

Barnes, J. S. *Fascism.* London: Thornton Butterworth, 1931.

Barnes, J. S. *The Universal Aspects of Fascism*. London: Williams and Norgate, 1928.

Bauer, Fritz. *Die Wurzeln faschistischen und national sozialistischen Handelns*. Frankfurt: Europäische Verlagsanstalt, 1965.

* De Felice, Renzo. *Le interpretazioni del fascismo*. Bari: Laterza, 1969.

*‡ Deutscher, Isaac, ed. *The Age of Permanent Revolution: A Trotsky Anthology*. New York: Dell, 1964. Especially chapter 10.

Drucker, Peter F. *The End of Economic Man: A Study of the New Totalitarianism*. London: Heinemann, 1939.

* Dutt, R. Palme. *Fascism and Social Revolution*, new ed. New York: International Publishers, 1935.

* Fetscher, Iring. "Faschismus und Nationalsozialismus: Zur Kritik des sowjetmarxistischen Faschismusbegriffs." *Politische Vierteljahrsschrift*, vol. III, no. 1 (March 1962), pp. 42–63.

*‡ Fromm, Erich. *Escape from Freedom*. New York: Holt, 1941.

* Guérin, Daniel. *Fascism and Big Business*. New York: Pioneer Publishers, 1939.

* Howe, Irving, ed. *The Basic Writings of Trotsky*. New York : Random House, 1963. Especially chapters 18–21.

* Lackō, Miclos. *Le Fascisme-Les Fascismes en Europe Centrale-Orientale*. Moscow: Editions "Naouka," 1970. (Report to the 13th International Congress of Historical Sciences, Moscow, August 16–23, 1970.)

* Laski, Harold J. *Reflections on the Revolution of Our Time*. New York: Viking, 1943.

*† Maruyama, Masao. *Thought and Behavior in Modern Japanese Politics*. New York: Oxford, 1963. Chapters 1–2, 4–5.

Maurras, Charles. *La Contre-Révolution spontanée: La recherche, la discussion, l'émeute, 1899–1939*. Lyon: H. Lardanchet, 1943.

*‡ Moore, Barrington, Jr. *Social Origins of Dictatorship and Democracy: Lord and Peasant in the Making of the Modern World*. Boston: Beacon Press, 1966.

†‡ Neumann, Sigmund. *Permanent Revolution: The Total State in a World at War*. New York: Harper, 1942.

*‡ Nolte, Ernst. *Three Faces of Fascism*. New York: Holt, Rinehart and Winston, 1966. Especially pp. 3–26, 455–62.

*† Nolte, Ernst, ed. *Theorien über den Faschismus*. Cologne/Berlin: Kiepenheuer and Witsch, 1967.

* Pirker, Theo, ed. *Komintern und Faschismus, 1920–1940*. Stuttgart, 1965. (Schriftenreihe der Vierteljahrshefte für Zeitgeschichte, no. 10.)

Rauschning, Hermann. *The Conservative Revolution.* New York: Putnam, 1941.

Rauschning, Hermann. *The Revolution of Nihilism: Warning to the West.* New York: Longmans, Green, 1939.

* Reich, Wilhelm. *The Mass Psychology of Fascism.* New York: Orgone Institute Press, 1946.

* Rogger, Hans. "Afterthoughts." In ‡ Rogger and Weber, eds., *The European Right,* pp. 575–89.

Sauer, Wolfgang. "National Socialism: Totalitarianism or Fascism?" *American Historical Review,* vol. LXXIII, no. 2 (December 1967), pp. 404–24.

Silone, Ignazio. *Der Fascismus: Seine Entstehung und seine Entwicklung.* Zurich: Europa Verlag, 1934.

* Weber, Eugen. "The Right: An Introduction." In ‡ Rogger and Weber, eds., *The European Right,* pp. 1–28.

† Whiteside, Andrew G. "The Nature and Origins of National Socialism." *Journal of Central European Affairs,* vol. XVII, no. 1 (April 1957), pp. 48–73.

* Vargas, Eugen. *The Great Crisis and Its Political Consequences: Economics and Politics, 1928–1934.* London: Modern Books, 1935.

*‡ Weiss, John. *The Fascist Tradition: Radical Right-Wing Extremism in Modern Europe.* New York: Harper, 1967.

CONCENTRATION CAMPS

Bettelheim, Bruno. *The Informed Heart: Autonomy in a Mass Age.* Glencoe, Ill.: The Free Press, 1960.

Billig, Joseph. *L'Hitlérisme et le système concentrationnaire.* Paris: Presses Universitaires, 1967.

† Devoto, Andrea. *Bibliografia dell'oppressione nazista fino al 1962.* Florence: Olschki, 1964.

‡ Hilberg, Raul. *The Destruction of the European Jews.* Chicago: Quadrangle Books, 1967.

*‡ Kogon, Eugen. *The Theory and Practice of Hell.* New York: Farrar, Straus, 1950.

‡ Reitlinger, Gerald. *The Final Solution: The Attempt to Exterminate the Jews of Europe, 1939–1945.* New York: A. S. Barnes, 1961.

Schnabel, Reimund, ed. *Macht ohne Moral: Dokumentation über die Moral.* Frankfurt: Röderbergverlag, 1957.

† Wormser-Migot, Olga. *Le Système concentrationnaire nazi, 1933–1945.* Paris: Presses Universitaires, 1968.

FASCISM IN ITALY

Alatri, Paolo. *Le origini del fascismo,* 4th ed. Rome: Riuniti, 1963.
*† Baer, George W. *The Coming of the Italian-Ethiopian War.* Cambridge, Mass.: Harvard University Press, 1967.
*† Bibes, Geneviève. "Le Fascisme italien: Etat des travaux depuis 1945." *Revue Française de Science Politique,* vol. XVIII, no. 6 (December 1968), pp. 1191–1245.
‡ Deakin, F. W. *The Brutal Friendship: Mussolini, Hitler, and the Fall of Italian Fascism.* New York: Harper, 1962.
De Felico, Renzo. *Mussolini il fascista.* Turin: Einaudi, 1966.
De Felico, Renzo. *Mussolini il rivoluzionario.* Turin: Einaudi, 1965.
Germino, Dante L. *The Italian Fascist Party in Power: A Study in Totalitarian Rule.* Minneapolis: University of Minnesota Press, 1959.
* Rossi, A. (Tasca, Angelo). *The Rise of Italian Fascism, 1918–1922.* London: Methuen, 1938. See also the latest and most complete Italian edition: *Nascita e avvento del fascismo* (Florence: La Nuova Italia, 1963).
Salvatorelli, Luigi, and Mira, Giovanni. *Storia d'Italia nel periodo fascista,* 5th ed. Turin: Einaudi, 1964.
* Salvemini, Gaetano. *The Fascist Dictatorship.* London: Jonathan Cape, 1928.
Santarelli, Enzo. *Storia del movimento e del regime fascista.* Rome: Riuniti, 1968.
* Togliatti, Palmiro. *Lezioni sul fascismo.* Rome: Riuniti, 1970.
Vivarelli, Roberto. *Il dopoguerra in Italia e l'avvento del fascismo, 1918–1922.* Naples: Instituto italiano per gli studi storici, 1967.
Webster, Richard A. *The Cross and the Fasces: Christian Democracy and Fascism in Italy.* Stanford: Stanford University Press, 1960.

FASCISM IN GERMANY

*‡ Allen, William S. *The Nazi Seizure of Power: The Experience of a Single German Town, 1930–1935.* Chicago: Quadrangle Books, 1965.
* Bracher, Karl Dietrich. *Die Auflösung der weimarer Republik,* 4th ed. Villingen: Ring Verlag, 1964.
*† Bracher, Karl Dietrich. *Die deutsche Diktatur: Entstehung, Struktur, Folgen des Nationalsozialismus.* Cologne/Berlin: Kiepenheuer and Witsch, 1969.

168   DYNAMICS OF COUNTERREVOLUTION

* Bracher, Karl Dietrich. Sauer, Wolfgang, and Schulz, Gerhard. *Die nationalsozialistische Machtergreifung*. Cologne: Westdeutscher Verlag, 1960.

Brady, Robert A. *The Spirit and Structure of German Fascism*. London: Victor Gollancz, 1937.

Brecht, Arnold. *Prelude to Silence: The End of the German Republic*. New York: Oxford, 1944.

*† Buchheim, Hans, Broszat, Martin, Jacobsen, Hans-Adolf, and Krausnick, Helmut. *Anatomie des SS-Staates*, 2 vols. Munich: Deutscher Taschenbuch Verlag, 1967.

‡ Bullock, Alan. *Hitler, A Study in Tyranny*, rev. ed. New York: Harper, 1964.

* Conway, J. S. *The Nazi Persecution of the Churches, 1933–1945*. New York: Basic Books, 1969.

Esenwein-Rothe, Ingeborg. *Die Wirtschaftsverbände von 1933–1945*. Berlin: Duncker, Humbolt, 1965.

Franz-Willing, Georg. *Die Hitlerbewegung: Der Ursprung, 1919–1922*. Hamburg: R. v. Decker's, 1962.

Hannover, H. and E. *Politische Justiz, 1918–1933*. Frankfurt: Fischer Bücherei, 1966.

* Heberle, Rudolf. *From Democracy to Nazism: A Regional Case Study in Political Parties in Germany*. Baton Rouge, La.: Louisiana State University, 1945.

Hoepke, Klaus-Peter. *Die deutsche Rechte und der italienische Faschismus*. Düsseldorf: Droste, 1968.

Jochmann, Werner. *Nationalsozialismus und Revolution: Ursprung und Geschichte der NSDAP in Hamburg*. Frankfurt, 1963.

Klein, Fritz. "Zur Vorbereitung der faschistischen Diktatur durch die deutsche Grossbourgeoisie, 1929–1932." *Zeitschrift für Geschichtswissenschaft*, vol. 1, no. 6 (1953), pp. 872–904.

Kruck, Alfred. *Geschichte des Alldeutschen Verbandes, 1890–1939*. Wiesbaden: Franz Steiner, 1954.

* Kühnl, Reinhard. *Die nationalsozialistische Linke, 1925–1930*. Meisenheim: Anton Hain, 1966.

Lepsius, M. Rainer. "The Collapse of an Intermediary Power Structure: Germany 1933–1934." *International Journal of Comparative Sociology*, vol. IX, nos. 3–4 (September and December 1968), pp. 289–301.

*‡ Lewy, Guenter. *The Catholic Church and Nazi Germany*. New York: McGraw-Hill, 1964.

Maser, Werner. *Die Frühgeschichte der NSDAP*. Frankfurt: Athenäum, 1965.

* Mason, T. W. "The Primacy of Politics: Politics and Economics in National Socialist Germany." In ‡ S. J. Woolf, ed.: *The Nature of Fascism* (New York: Random House, 1968), pp. 165–95.

* Mason, T. W. "Some Origins of the Second World War" *Past and Present*, No. 29 (December 1964), pp. 67–87.

* Matthias, Erich, and Morsey, Rudolf, ed. *Das Ende der Parteien: 1933*. Düsseldorf: Droste, 1960.

Messerschmidt, Manfred. *Die Wehrmacht im NS-Staat: Zeit der Indoktrination*. Hamburg: R. v. Decker's, 1969.

Mohler, Armin. *Die konservative Revolution in Deutschland, 1918–1932*. Stuttgart: Friedrich Vorwerk, 1950.

* Mommsen, Hans. *Beamtentum im Dritten Reich*. Berlin: Deutsche Verlags-Anstalt, 1966.

*‡ Neumann, Franz L. *Behemoth: The Structure and Practice of National Socialism*, 2d ed. New York: Oxford, 1944.

O'Neill, Robert J. *The German Army and the Nazi Party, 1933–1939*. London: Cassell, 1966.

*‡ Schoenbaum, David. *Hitler's Social Revolution: Class and Status in Nazi Germany, 1933–1939*. Garden City, N.Y.: Doubleday, 1966.

* Schweitzer, Arthur. *Big Business in the Third Reich*. Bloomington, Ind.: Indiana University Press, 1964.

Sontheimer, Kurt. *Antidemokratisches Denken in der weimarer Republik: Die politischen Ideen des deutschen Nationalismus zwischen 1918 und 1933*. Munich: Nymphenburger Verlag, 1962.

Trial of the German Major War Criminals. London, 1946–1950.

Trial of the Major War Criminals before the International Military Tribunal. 42 vols. Nuremberg, 1947–1949.

‡ Wheeler-Bennett, John W. *The Nemesis of Power: The German Army in Politics, 1918–1945*. New York: St. Martin's Press, 1954.

*‡ Zahn, Gordon. *German Catholics and Hitler's Wars*. London: Sheed and Ward, 1962.

SPAIN

Broué, Pierre, and Témine, Emile. *La Révolution et la guerre d'Espagne*. Paris: Minuit, 1961.

† Carr, Raymond. *Spain, 1808–1939*. Oxford: Clarendon, 1966.

† Cierva Y De Hoces, Ricardo de la, ed. *Bibliografía general sobre la Guerra de Espana (1936–1939) y sus antecedentes historicos*. Madrid, 1968.

‡ Jackson, Gabriel. *The Spanish Republic and the Civil War, 1931–1939*. Princeton: Princeton University Press, 1965.

* Nellessen, Bernd. *Die verbotene Revolution: Aufstieg und Niedergang der Falange.* Hamburg: Leipniz, 1963.

‡ Payne, Stanley G. *Falange: A History of Spanish Fascism.* Stanford: Stanford University Press, 1961.

Puzzo, Dante A. *Spain and the Great Powers, 1936–1941.* New York: Columbia University Press, 1962.

AUSTRIA

† Benedikt, Heinrich ed. *Geschichte der Republik Österreich.* Vienna: Verlag für Geschichte und Politik, 1954.

Gulick, C. A. *Austria: From Habsburg to Hitler,* 2 vols. Berkeley: University of California Press, 1948.

Hofmann, Josef. *Der Pfrimer-Putsch.* Graz, 1965.

Jedlicka, Ludwig F., ed. *Die Erhebung der österreichischen Nationalsozialisten im July 1934.* Vienna: Europa Verlag, 1965.

Jedlicka, Ludwig F., ed. *Ein Heer im Schatten der Parteien: die militärpolitische Lage Österreichs, 1918–1938.* Graz: H. Böhlaus, 1955.

Reimann, Viktor. *Zu gross für Österreich: Seipel und Bauer im Kampf um die erste Republik.* Vienna: Molden, 1968.

Schuschnigg, Kurt. *Austrian Requiem.* New York: Putnam, 1946.

———. *My Austria.* New York: Knopf, 1938.

Stadler, Karl. *Österreich 1938–1945: Im Spiegel der Ns-Akten.* Munich: Herold, 1967.

Starhemberg, E. R. *Between Hitler and Mussolini.* New York: Harper, 1942.

FRANCE

Aron, Robert. *Histoire de l'Épuration,* 2 vols. Paris: Fayard, 1967–1969.

Chavardès, Maurice. *Le 6 février 1934: La république en danger.* Paris: Calmann-Lévy, 1966.

LeClère, Marcel. *Le 6 février.* Paris: Hachette, 1967.

Cotta, Michèle. *La Collaboration, 1940–1944.* Paris: Colin, 1964.

Delperrie De Bayac, J. *Histoire de la Milice, 1918–1945.* Paris: Fayard, 1969.

Girardet, Raoul. "Notes sur l'Esprit d'un fascisme français, 1934–1939." *Revue Française de Science Politique,* vol. V, no. 3 (July-September 1955), pp. 529–46.

* Hoffmann, Stanley. "Collaborationism in France During World War II." *Journal of Modern History,* vol. 40, no. 3 (September 1968), pp. 375–95.

* Micaud, Charles. *The French Right and Nazi Germany, 1933–1939: A Study of Public Opinion.* Durham: Duke University Press, 1943.

† Novak, Peter. *The Resistance versus Vichy: The Purge of Collaborators in Liberated France.* New York: Columbia University Press, 1968.

Paxton, Robert. *Parades and Politics at Vichy: The French Officers Corps under Marshal Pétain.* Princeton: Princeton University Press, 1966.

Plumyène, J. and Lasierra, R. *Les Fascismes français, 1923–1963.* Paris: Seuil, 1963.

* Rémond, René. *La Droite en France,* new ed. Paris: Aubier, 1963.

Rudaux, Philippe. *Les Croix de Feu et le P.S.F.* Paris: France-Empire, 1967.

Saint-Paulien (Sicard, M. Y.). *Histoire de la Collaboration.* Paris: L'Esprit Nouveau, 1964.

‡ Weber, Eugen. *Action Française: Royalism and Reaction in Twentieth-Century France.* Stanford: Stanford University Press, 1962.

Weber, Eugen. "Nationalism, Socialism, and National-Socialism in France." *French Historical Studies,* vol. II, no. 3 (Spring 1962), pp. 273–307.

Wolf, Dieter. *Die Doriot-Bewegung.* Stuttgart: Deutsche Verlagsanstalt, 1967.

ENGLAND

Cross, Colin. *The Fascists in Britain.* New York: St. Martin's, 1963.

* George, Margaret. *The Warped Vision: British Foreign Policy, 1933–1939.* Pittsburgh: University of Pittsburgh Press, 1965.

‡ Gilbert, Martin and Gott, Richard. *The Appeasers.* London: Weidenfeld and Nicolson, 1963.

Jones, Thomas. *A Diary With Letters.* London: Oxford, 1954.

* Rowse, A. L. *All Souls and Appeasement: A Contribution to Contemporary History.* London: Macmillan, 1961.

BELGIUM

Baes, R. *Joris van Severen: Une Ame.* Zulte: Editions Oranje, 1966 [?].

Etienne, Jean-Michel. *Le Mouvement Rexiste jusqu'en 1940.* Paris: Colin, 1968.

HOLLAND

Mason, Henry L. *The Purge of Dutch Quislings.* The Hague: Martinus Nijhoff, 1962.

Warmbrunn, Werner. *The Dutch Under German Occupation.* Stanford: Stanford University Press, 1963.

EASTERN EUROPE AND BALKANS

* Broszat, Martin. "Faschismus und Kollaboration in Ostmitteleuropa zwischen den Weltkriegen." "Vierteljahrshefte für Zeitgeschichte, vol. 14, no. 3 (July 1966), pp. 225–51.

Cliadakis, Harry. *Greek Fascism, 1935–1941: The Metaxas Regime and the Coming of World War II.* Unpublished Ph.D. thesis, New York University, 1970.

Deák, Istaván. "Hungary." In ‡ Rogger and Weber, eds. *The European Right*, pp. 364–407.

Macartney, C. A. *October Fifteenth: A History of Modern Hungary, 1929–1945*, 2 vols., 2d ed. Edinburgh: University Press, 1961.

† Macartney, C. A., and Palmer, A. W. *Independent Eastern Europe.* London: Macmillan, 1962.

Prost, Henri. *Destin de la Roumanie.* Paris: Berger-Levrault, 1954.

Rintala, Marvin. *Three Generations: The Extreme Right Wing in Finnish Politics.* Bloomington, Ind.: Indiana University Press, 1962.

Roberts, Henry L. *Rumania: Political Problems of an Agrarian State.* New Haven: Yale University Press, 1951.

* Roos, Hans. *A History of Modern Poland: From the Foundation of the State in the First World War to the Present Day.* New York: Knopf, 1966.

Rothschild, Joseph. *Pilsudski's Coup d'Etat.* New York: Columbia University Press, 1966.

‡ Seton-Watson, Hugh. *Eastern Europe Between the Wars, 1918–1941.* Cambridge: Cambridge University Press, 1945.

Szinai, Miklós, and Szücs, László, eds. *Confidential Papers of Admiral Horthy.* Budapest: Corvina, 1965.

RESISTANCE

† Battaglia, Roberto. *Storia della resistenza italiana*, 2d ed. Turin: Einaudi, 1964.

†‡ Delzell, Charles F. *Mussolini's Enemies: The Italian Anti-Fascist Resistance.* Princeton: Princeton University Press, 1961.

* *European Resistance Movements, 1939–1945.* Proceedings of the First and Second International Conference on the History of the Resistance Movements, 2 vols. New York: Pergamon Press, 1960–1964.

* Graml, H., Mommsen, H., Reichhardt, H.-J., and Wolf, E. *The German Resistance to Hitler.* Berkeley: University of California Press, 1970.

Kuhnrich, Heinz. *Der Partisanenkrieg in Europa, 1939–1945.* Berlin: Dietz Verlag, 1968.

Loverdo, Costa de. *Les Maquis rouges des Balkans, 1941–1945: Grèce-Yougoslavie-Albanie.* Paris: Stock, 1967.

*Michel, Henri. *Les Mouvements clandestins en Europe,* 2d ed. Paris: Presses Universitaires, 1965.

Vistel, Alban. *La Nuit sans ombre.* Paris: Fayard, 1970.

Japan

Brown, Delmer M. *Nationalism in Japan.* Berkeley: University of California Press, 1955.

‡ Butow, Robert J. *Japan's Decision to Surrender.* Stanford: Stanford University Press, 1954.

Byas, Hugh: *Government By Assassination.* New York: Knopf, 1942.

Crowley, James B. *Japan's Quest for Autonomy: National Security and Foreign Policy, 1930–1938.* Princeton: Princeton University Press, 1966.

Maxon, Y. C. *Control of Japanese Foreign Policy.* Berkeley: University of California Press, 1957.

Morley, James W. "The First Seven Weeks." *The Japan Interpreter,* vol. VI, no. 2 (Summer 1970), pp. 151–64.

Scalapino, Robert A. *Democracy and the Party Movement in Prewar Japan: The Failure of the First Attempt.* Berkeley: University of California Press, 1953.

Storry, Richard. *The Double Patriots: A Study of Japanese Nationalism.* Boston: Houghton Mifflin, 1957.

* Tanin, O., and Yohan, E. *Militarism and Fascism in Japan.* New York: International Publishers, 1934. Including an important introduction by Karl Radek, pp. 7–22.

Wilson, George M. "A New Look at the Problem of 'Japanese Fascism.'" *Comparative Studies in Society and History,* vol. X, no. 4 (July 1968), pp. 401–12.

Wilson, George M. *Radical Nationalist in Japan: Kita Ikki, 1883–1937.* Cambridge, Mass.: Harvard University Press, 1969.

hARPER ✦ ᴛORChBOOKS

American Studies: General

HENRY ADAMS Degradation of the Democratic Dogma. ‡ *Introduction by Charles Hirschfeld.* TB/1450

LOUIS D. BRANDEIS: Other People's Money, *and How the Bankers Use It. Ed. with Intro, by Richard M. Abrams* TB/3081

HENRY STEELE COMMAGER, Ed.: The Struggle for Racial Equality TB/1300

CARL N. DEGLER: Out of Our Past: *The Forces that Shaped Modern America* CN/2

CARL N. DEGLER, Ed.: Pivotal Interpretations of American History
Vol. I TB/1240; Vol. II TB/1241

LAWRENCE H. FUCHS, Ed.: American Ethnic Politics TB/1368

ROBERT L. HEILBRONER: The Limits of American Capitalism TB/1305

JOHN HIGHAM, Ed.: The Reconstruction of American History TB/1068

ROBERT H. JACKSON: The Supreme Court in the American System of Government TB/1106

JOHN F. KENNEDY: A Nation of Immigrants. *Illus. Revised and Enlarged. Introduction by Robert F. Kennedy* TB/1118

RICHARD B. MORRIS: Fair Trial: *Fourteen Who Stood Accused, from Anne Hutchinson to Alger Hiss* TB/1335

GUNNAR MYRDAL: An American Dilemma: *The Negro Problem and Modern Democracy. Introduction by the Author.*
Vol. I TB/1443; Vol. II TB/1444

GILBERT OSOFSKY, Ed.: The Burden of Race: *A Documentary History of Negro-White Relations in America* TB/1405

ARNOLD ROSE: The Negro in America: *The Condensed Version of Gunnar Myrdal's* An American Dilemma. *Second Edition* TB/3048

JOHN E. SMITH: Themes in American Philosophy: *Purpose, Experience and Community* TB/1466

WILLIAM R. TAYLOR: Cavalier and Yankee: *The Old South and American National Character* TB/1474

American Studies: Colonial

BERNARD BAILYN: The New England Merchants in the Seventeenth Century TB/1149

ROBERT E. BROWN: Middle-Class Democracy and Revolution in Massachusetts, 1691–1780. *New Introduction by Author* TB/1413

JOSEPH CHARLES: The Origins of the American Party System TB/1049

WESLEY FRANK CRAVEN: The Colonies in Transition: 1660-1712† TB/3084

CHARLES GIBSON: Spain in America † TB/3077

CHARLES GIBSON, Ed.: The Spanish Tradition in America + HR/1351

LAWRENCE HENRY GIPSON: The Coming of the Revolution: 1763-1775. † *Illus.* TB/3007

JACK P. GREENE, Ed.: Great Britain and the American Colonies: 1606-1763. + *Introduction by the Author* HR/1477

AUBREY C. LAND, Ed.: Bases of the Plantation Society + HR/1429

PERRY MILLER: Errand Into the Wilderness TB/1139

PERRY MILLER & T. H. JOHNSON, Ed.: The Puritans: *A Sourcebook of Their Writings*
Vol. I TB/1093; Vol. II TB/1094

EDMUND S. MORGAN: The Puritan Family: *Religion and Domestic Relations in Seventeenth Century New England* TB/1227

WALLACE NOTESTEIN: The English People on the Eve of Colonization: 1603-1630. † *Illus.* TB/3006

LOUIS B. WRIGHT: The Cultural Life of the American Colonies: 1607-1763. † *Illus.* TB/3005

YVES F. ZOLTVANY, Ed.: The French Tradition in America + HR/1425

American Studies: The Revolution to 1860

JOHN R. ALDEN: The American Revolution: 1775-1783. † *Illus.* TB/3011

RAY A. BILLINGTON: The Far Western Frontier: 1830-1860. † *Illus.* TB/3012

STUART BRUCHEY: The Roots of American Economic Growth, 1607-1861: *An Essay in Social Causation. New Introduction by the Author.* TB/1350

NOBLE E. CUNNINGHAM, JR., Ed.: The Early Republic, 1789-1828 + HR/1394

GEORGE DANGERFIELD: The Awakening of American Nationalism, 1815-1828. † *Illus.* TB/3061

---

† The New American Nation Series, edited by Henry Steele Commager and Richard B. Morris.
‡ American Perspectives series, edited by Bernard Wishy and William E. Leuchtenburg.
α History of Europe series, edited by J. H. Plumb.
§ The Library of Religion and Culture, edited by Benjamin Nelson.
‖ Researches in the Social, Cultural, and Behavioral Sciences, edited by Benjamin Nelson.
Σ Harper Modern Science Series, edited by James A. Newman.
° Not for sale in Canada.
+ Documentary History of the United States series, edited by Richard B. Morris.
# Documentary History of Western Civilization series, edited by Eugene C. Black and Leonard W. Levy.
∧ The Economic History of the United States series, edited by Henry David et al.
¶ European Perspectives series, edited by Eugene C. Black.
** Contemporary Essays series, edited by Leonard W. Levy.
* The Stratum Series, edited by John Hale.

H. R. TREVOR-ROPER: The European Witch-craze of the Sixteenth and Seventeenth Centuries and Other Essays ° TB/1416
VESPASIANO: Rennaissance Princes, Popes, and XVth Century: The Vespasiano Memoirs. Introduction by Myron P. Gilmore. Illus. TB/1111

History: Modern European

MAX BELOFF: The Age of Absolutism, 1660-1815 TB/1062
D. W. BROGAN: The Development of Modern France ° Vol. I: From the Fall of the Empire to the Dreyfus Affair TB/1184
Vol. II: The Shadow of War, World War I, Between the Two Wars TB/1185
ALAN BULLOCK: Hitler, A Study in Tyranny. ° Revised Edition. Illus. TB/1123
JOHANN GOTTLIEB FICHTE: Addresses to the German Nation. Ed. with Intro. by George A. Kelly ¶ TB/1366
ALBERT GOODWIN: The French Revolution TB/1064
H. STUART HUGHES: The Obstructed Path: French Social Thought in the Years of Desperation TB/1451
JOHAN HUIZINGA: Dutch Civilization in the 17th Century and Other Essays TB/1453
JOHN MCMANNERS: European History, 1789-1914: Men, Machines and Freedom TB/1419
FRANZ NEUMANN: Behemoth: The Structure and Practice of National Socialism, 1933-1944 TB/1289
DAVID OGG: Europe of the Ancien Régime, 1715-1783 ° α TB/1271
ALBERT SOREL: Europe Under the Old Regime. Translated by Francis H. Herrick TB/1121
A. J. P. TAYLOR: From Napoleon to Lenin: Historical Essays ° TB/1268
A. J. P. TAYLOR: The Habsburg Monarchy, 1809-1918: A History of the Austrian Empire and Austria-Hungary ° TB/1187
J. M. THOMPSON: European History, 1494-1789 TB/1431
H. R. TREVOR-ROPER: Historical Essays TB/1269

Literature & Literary Criticism

JACQUES BARZUN: The House of Intellect TB/1051
W. J. BATE: From Classic to Romantic: Premises of Taste in Eighteenth Century England TB/1036
VAN WYCK BROOKS: Van Wyck Brooks: The Early Years: A Selection from his Works, 1908-1921 Ed. with Intro. by Claire Sprague TB/3082
RICHMOND LATTIMORE, Translator: The Odyssey of Homer TB/1389

Philosophy

HENRI BERGSON: Time and Free Will: An Essay on the Immediate Data of Consciousness ° TB/1021
H. J. BLACKHAM: Six Existentialist Thinkers: Kierkegaard, Nietzsche, Jaspers, Marcel, Heidegger, Sartre ° TB/1002
J. M. BOCHENSKI: The Methods of Contemporary Thought. Trans by Peter Caws TB/1377
CRANE BRINTON: Nietzsche. Preface, Bibliography, and Epilogue by the Author TB/1197
ERNST CASSIRER: Rousseau, Kant and Goethe. Intro by Peter Gay TB/1092
WILFRID DESAN: The Tragic Finale: An Essay on the Philosophy of Jean-Paul Sartre TB/1030

MARVIN FARBER: The Aims of Phenomenology: The Motives, Methods, and Impact of Husserl's Thought TB/1291
PAUL FRIEDLANDER: Plato: An Introduction TB/2017
MICHAEL GELVEN: A Commentary on Heidegger's "Being and Time" TB/1464
G. W. F. HEGEL: On Art, Religion Philosophy: Introductory Lectures to the Realm of Absolute Spirit. || Edited with an Introduction by J. Glenn Gray TB/1463
G. W. F. HEGEL: Phenomenology of Mind. ° || Introduction by eGorge Lichtheim TB/1303
MARTIN HEIDEGGER: Discourse on Thinking. Translated with a Preface by John M. Anderson and E. Hans Freund. Introduction by John M. Anderson TB/1459
F. H. HEINEMANN: Existentialism and the Modern Predicament TB/28
WERER HEISENBERG: Physics and Philosophy: The Revolution in Modern Science. Intro. by F. S. C. Northrop TB/549
EDMUND HUSSERL: Phenomenology and the Crisis of Philosophy. § Translated with an Introduction by Quentin Lauer · TB/1170
IMMANUEL KANT: Groundwork of the Metaphysic of Morals. Translated and Analyzed by H. J. Paton TB/1159
IMMANUEL KANT: Lectures on Ethics. § Introduction by Lewis White Beck TB/105
QUENTIN LAUER: Phenomenology: Its Genesis and Prospect. Preface by Aron Gurwitsch TB/1169
GEORGE A. MORGAN: What Nietzsche Means TB/1198
H. J. PATON: The Categorical Imperative: A Study in Kant's Moral Philosophy TB/1325
MICHAEL POLANYI: Personal Knowledge: Towards a Post-Critical Philosophy TB/1158
WILLARD VAN ORMAN QUINE: Elementary Logic Revised Edition TB/577
JOHN E. SMITH: Themes in American Philosophy: Purpose, Experience and Community TB/1466
MORTON WHITE: Foundations of Historical Knowledge TB/1440
WILHELM WINDELBAND: A History of Philosophy Vol. I: Greek, Roman, Medieval TB/38
Vol. II: Renaissance, Enlightenment, Modern TB/39
LUDWIG WITTGENSTEIN: The Blue and Brown Books ° TB/1211
LUDWIG WITTGENSTEIN: Notebooks, 1914-1916 TB/1441

Political Science & Government

C. E. BLACK: The Dynamics of Modernization: A Study in Comparative History TB/1321
KENNETH E. BOULDING: Conflict and Defense: A General Theory of Action TB/3024
DENIS W. BROGAN: Politics in America. New Introduction by the Author TB/1469
LEWIS COSER, Ed.: Political Sociology TB/1293
ROBERT A. DAHL & CHARLES E. LINDBLOM: Politics, Economics, and Welfare: Planning and Politico-Economic Systems Resolved into Basic Social Processes TB/3037
ROY C. MACRIDIS, Ed.: Political Parties: Contemporary Trends and Ideas ** TB/1322
ROBERT GREEN MC CLOSKEY: American Conservatism in the Age of Enterprise, 1865-1910 TB/1137
JOHN B. MORRALL: Political Thought in Medieval Times TB/1076

4

KARL R. POPPER: The Open Society and Its
Enemies *Vol. I: The Spell of Plato* TB/1101
*Vol. II: The High Tide of Prophecy: Hegel,
Marx, and the Aftermath* TB/1102
HENRI DE SAINT-SIMON: Social Organization, The
Science of Man, and Other Writings. ||
*Edited and Translated with an Introduction
by Felix Markham* TB/1152
JOSEPH A. SCHUMPETER: Capitalism, Socialism
and Democracy TB/3008

Psychology

LUDWIG BINSWANGER: Being-in-the-World: *Se-
lected Papers.* || *Trans. with Intro. by Jacob
Needleman* TB/1365
HADLEY CANTRIL: The Invasion from Mars: *A
Study in the Psychology of Panic* || TB/1282
MIRCEA ELIADE: Cosmos and History: *The Myth
of the Eternal Return* § TB/2050
MIRCEA ELIADE: Myth and Reality TB/1369
MIRCEA ELIADE: Myths, Dreams and Mysteries:
*The Encounter Between Contemporary Faiths
and Archaic Realities* § TB/1320
MIRCEA ELIADE: Rites and Symbols of Initiation:
The Mysteries of Birth and Rebirth §
TB/1236
SIGMUND FREUD: On Creativity and the Uncon-
scious: *Papers on the Psychology of Art,
Literature, Love, Religion.* § *Intro. by Ben-
jamin Nelson* TB/45
J. GLENN GRAY: The Warriors: *Reflections on
Men in Battle. Introduction by Hannah
Arendt* TB/1294
WILLIAM JAMES: Psychology: *The Briefer
Course. Edited with an Intro. by Gordon
Allport* TB/1034
KARL MENNINGER, M.D.: Theory of Psychoan-
alytic Technique TB/1144

Religion: Ancient and Classical, Biblical and Judaic Traditions

MARTIN BUBER: Eclipse of God: *Studies in the
Relation Between Religion and Philosophy*
TB/12
MARTIN BUBER: Hasidism and Modern Man.
Edited and Translated by Maurice Friedman
TB/839
MARTIN BUBER: The Knowledge of Man. *Edited
with an Introduction by Maurice Friedman.
Translated by Maurice Friedman and Ronald
Gregor Smith* TB/135
MARTIN BUBER: Moses. *The Revelation and the
Covenant* TB/837
MARTIN BUBER: The Origin and Meaning of
Hasidism. *Edited and Translated by Maurice
Friedman* TB/835
MARTIN BUBER: The Prophetic Faith TB/73
MARTIN BUBER: Two Types of Faith: *Interpene-
tration of Judaism and Christianity* ° TB/75
MALCOLM L. DIAMOND: Martin Buber: *Jewish
Existentialist* TB/840
M. S. ENSLIN: Christian Beginnings TB/5
M. S. ENSLIN: The Literature of the Christian
Movement TB/6
HENRI FRANKFORT: Ancient Egyptian Religion:
An Interpretation TB/77
ABRAHAM HESCHEL: God in Search of Man: *A
Philosophy of Judaism* TB/807
ABRAHAM HESCHEL: Man Is not Alone: *A Phil-
osophy of Religion* TB/838
T. J. MEEK: Hebrew Origins TB/69
H. J. ROSE: Religion in Greece and Rome
TB/55

Religion: Early Christianity Through Reformation

ANSELM OF CANTERBURY: Truth, Freedom, and
Evil: *Three Philosophical Dialogues. Edited
and Translated by Jasper Hopkins and Her-
bert Richardson* TB/317
JOHANNES ECKHART: Meister Eckhart: *A Mod-
ern Translation by R. Blakney* TB/8
EDGAR J. GOODSPEED: A Life of Jesus TB/1
ROBERT M. GRANT: Gnosticism and Early Christi-
anity TB/136
ARTHUR DARBY NOCK: St. Paul ° TR/104
GORDON RUPP: Luther's Progress to the Diet of
Worms ° TB/120

Religion: The Protestant Tradition

KARL BARTH: Church Dogmatics: *A Selection.
Intro. by H. Gollwitzer. Ed. by G. W. Bro-
miley* TB/95
KARL BARTH: Dogmatics in Outline TB/56
KARL BARTH: The Word of God and the Word
of Man TB/13
WILLIAM R. HUTCHISON, Ed.: American Prot-
estant Thought: *The Liberal Era* ‡ TB/1385
SOREN KIERKEGAARD: Edifying Discourses. *Edited
with an Intro. by Paul Holmer* TB/32
SOREN KIERKEGAARD: The Journals of Kierke-
gaard. ° *Edited with an Intro. by Alexander
Dru* TB/52
SOREN KIERKEGAARD: The Point of View for My
Work as an Author: *A Report to History.* §
Preface by Benjamin Nelson TB/88
SOREN KIERKEGAARD: The Present Age. § *Trans-
lated and edited by Alexander Dru. Intro-
duction by Walter Kaufmann* TB/94
SOREN KIERKEGAARD: Purity of Heart. *Trans. by
Douglas Steere* TB/4
SOREN KIERKEGAARD: Repetition: *An Essay in
Experimental Psychology* § TB/117
WOLFHART PANNENBERG, et al.: History and Her-
meneutic. *Volume 4 of Journal for Theol-
ogy and the Church, edited by Robert W.
Funk and Gerhard Ebeling* TB/254
F. SCHLEIERMACHER: The Christian Faith. *Intro-
duction by Richard R. Niebuhr.*
Vol. I TB/108; Vol. II TB/109
F. SCHLEIERMACHER: On Religion: *Speeches to
Its Cultured Despisers. Intro. by Rudolf
Otto* TB/36
PAUL TILLICH: Dynamics of Faith TB/42
PAUL TILLICH: Morality and Beyond TB/142

Religion: The Roman & Eastern Christian Traditions

A. ROBERT CAPONIGRI, Ed.: Modern Catholic
Thinkers II: *The Church and the Political
Order* TB/307
G. P. FEDOTOV: The Russian Religious Mind:
*Kievan Christianity, the tenth to the thir-
teenth Centuries* TB/370
GABRIEL MARCEL: Being and Having: *An Ex-
istential Diary. Introduction by James Col-
lins* TB/310
GABRIEL MARCEL: Homo Viator: *Introduction to
a Metaphysic of Hope* TB/397

Religion: Oriental Religions

TOR ANDRAE: Mohammed: *The Man and His
Faith* § TB/62
EDWARD CONZE: Buddhism: *Its Essence and De-
velopment.* ° *Foreword by Arthur Waley*
TB/58

EDWARD CONZE et al, Editors: Buddhist Texts
through the Ages TB/113
H. G. CREEL: Confucius and the Chinese Way
TB/63
FRANKLIN EDGERTON, Trans. & Ed.: The Bhaga-
vad Gita TB/115
SWAMI NIKHILANANDA, Trans. & Ed.: The
Upanishads TB/114

Religion: Philosophy, Culture, and Society

NICOLAS BERDYAEV: The Destiny of Man TB/61
RUDOLF BULTMANN: History and Eschatology:
The Presence of Eternity ° TB/91
LUDWIG FEUERBACH: The Essence of Christianity.
§ Introduction by Karl Barth. Foreword by
H. Richard Niebuhr TB/11
ADOLF HARNACK: What Is Christianity? § Intro-
duction by Rudolf Bultmann TB/17
KYLE HASELDEN: The Racial Problem in Chris-
tian Perspective TB/116
IMMANUEL KANT: Religion Within the Limits of
Reason Alone. § Introduction by Theodore
M. Greene and John Silber TB/67
H. RICHARD NIEBUHR: Christ and Culture TB/3
H. RICHARD NIEBUHR: The Kingdom of God in
America TB/49

Science and Mathematics

W. E. LE GROS CLARK: The Antecedents of
Man: An Introduction to the Evolution of
the Primates. ° Illus. TB/559
ROBERT E. COKER: Streams, Lakes, Ponds. Illus.
TB/586
ROBERT E. COKER: This Great and Wide Sea: An
Introduction to Oceanography and Marine
Biology. Illus. TB/551
F. K. HARE: The Restless Atmosphere TB/560
WILLARD VAN ORMAN QUINE: Mathematical Logic
TB/558

Science: Philosophy

J. M. BOCHENSKI: The Methods of Contempor-
ary Thought. Tr. by Peter Caws TB/1377
J. BRONOWSKI: Science and Human Values. Re-
vised and Enlarged. Illus. TB/505
WERNER HEISENBERG: Physics and Philosophy:
The Revolution in Modern Science. Introduc-
tion by F. S. C. Northrop TB/549
KARL R. POPPER: Conjectures and Refutations:
The Growth of Scientific Knowledge TB/1376
KARL R. POPPER: The Logic of Scientific Dis-
covery TB/576

Sociology and Anthropology

REINHARD BENDIX: Work and Authority in In-
dustry: Ideologies of Management in the
Course of Industrialization TB/3035
BERNARD BERELSON, Ed., The Behavioral Sci-
ences Today TB/1127
KENNETH B. CLARK: Dark Ghetto: Dilemmas of
Social Power. Foreword by Gunnar Myrdal
TB/1317

KENNETH CLARK & JEANNETTE HOPKINS: A Rele-
vant War Against Poverty: A Study of Com-
munity Action Programs and Observable So-
cial Change TB/1480
LEWIS COSER, Ed.: Political Sociology TB/1293
ALLISON DAVIS & JOHN DOLLARD: Children of
Bondage: The Personality Development of
Negro Youth in the Urban South ‖ TB/3049
ST. CLAIR DRAKE & HORACE R. CAYTON: Black
Metropolis: A Study of Negro Life in a
Northern City. Introduction by Everett C.
Hughes. Tables, maps, charts, and graphs
Vol. I TB/1086; Vol. II TB/1087
PETER F. DRUCKER: The New Society: The Anat-
omy of Industrial Order TB/1082
CHARLES Y. GLOCK & RODNEY STARK: Christian
Beliefs and Anti-Semitism. Introduction by
the Authors TB/1454
ALVIN W. GOULDNER: The Hellenic World
TB/1479
R. M. MACIVER: Social Causation TB/1153
GARY T. MARX: Protest and Prejudice: A Study
of Belief in the Black Community TB/1435
ROBERT K. MERTON, LEONARD BROOM, LEONARD S.
COTTRELL, JR., Editors: Sociology Today:
Problems and Prospects ‖
Vol. I TB/1173; Vol. II TB/1174
GILBERT OSOFSKY, Ed.: The Burden of Race: A
Documentary History of Negro-White Rela-
tions in America TB/1405
GILBERT OSOFSKY: Harlem: The Making of a
Ghetto: Negro New York 1890-1930 TB/1381
TALCOTT PARSONS & EDWARD A. SHILS, Editors:
Toward a General Theory of Action: Theo-
retical Foundations for the Social Sciences
TB/1083
PHILIP RIEFF: The Triumph of the Therapeutic:
Uses of Faith After Freud TB/1360
JOHN H. ROHRER & MUNRO S. EDMONSON, Eds.:
The Eighth Generation Grows Up: Cultures
and Personalities of New Orleans Negroes ‖
TB/3050
ARNOLD ROSE: The Negro in America: The Con-
densed Version of Gunnar Myrdal's An
American Dilemma. Second Edition TB/3048
GEORGE ROSEN: Madness in Society: Chapters in
the Historical Sociology of Mental Illness. ‖
Preface by Benjamin Nelson TB/1337
PHILIP SELZNICK: TVA and the Grass Roots:
A Study in the Sociology of Formal Organi-
zation TB/1230
PITIRIM A. SOROKIN: Contemporary Sociological
Theories: Through the First Quarter of the
Twentieth Century TB/3046
MAURICE R. STEIN: The Eclipse of Community:
An Interpretation of American Studies
TB/1128
FERDINAND TONNIES: Community and Society:
Gemeinschaft und Gesellschaft. Translated
and Edited by Charles P. Loomis TB/1116
W. LLOYD WARNER and Associates: Democracy
in Jonesville: A Study in Quality and In-
equality ‖ TB/1129
W. LLOYD WARNER: Social Class in America:
The Evaluation of Status TB/1013
FLORIAN ZNANIECKI: The Social Role of the
Man of Knowledge. Introduction by Lewis
A. Coser TB/1372